Introduction 4

Lucifer 6

Beelzebub 8

Leviathan 10

Baal 12

Asmodeus 14

Abaddon 16

Mammon 18

Belphegor 20

Samael 22

Lilith 24

Astaroth 26

Belial 28

Pazuzu 30

Baphomet 32

Vine 34

Andras 36

Furfur 38

Malphas 40

Marchosias 42

Zagan 44

Aamon 46

Stolas 48

Orobas 50

Vepar 52

Introduction

Welcome to the arcane and mesmerizing world of "Tattoo Design Book-Demonology." Within these pages lies a collection unlike any other, where the profound depths of ancient mythologies and the piercing truths of existential symbolism are etched into the very fabric of reality through the art of tattooing. This book presents twenty-four demons, each meticulously selected not only for their aesthetic appeal but also for the rich narratives and symbolic power they embody. These are not mere illustrations; they are gateways to a deeper understanding of the dark, the divine, and the duality of human nature.

The Essence of the Infernal

The demons featured in this volume range from the notorious architects of hell's grandiose schemes to the enigmatic guardians of forgotten truths. Each demon's portrayal is more than just an image; it is an invitation to explore complex themes such as morality, chaos, wisdom, and transformation. These beings, often misunderstood and misrepresented throughout history, are presented here in their most authentic forms, drawn from the depths of various cultural wellsprings.

Why Demons?

In every culture, demons have held a place in folklore as embodiments of challenges or as metaphysical explanations for the natural and moral order of the universe. In modern contexts, they represent personal and communal struggles, symbolizing battles that are both internally psychic and externally chaotic. A tattoo of a demon can serve as a personal talisman, a reminder of one's endurance through hardship, or a mark of respect for the primal forces that shape the world.

Artistic Interpretations

The artistic interpretations in "Infernal Ink" are inspired by traditional and contemporary styles, from stark blackwork to vibrant watercolors. Each demon is depicted with attention to detail that respects their mythological roots while incorporating modern tattoo aesthetics. The imagery of Astaroth's scholarly might, the fierce loyalty of Marchosias, or the dual nature of Baphomet are crafted not only to captivate and adorn but to provoke thought and reflection.

Guidance for the Seeker

For those considering embodying these symbols on their skin, this book serves as a guide not only to the artistic and aesthetic considerations but also to the ethical and spiritual dimensions. Choosing to wear a demon permanently is a powerful statement, one that carries depth beyond the ink and skin, resonating with the energies of ancient tales and personal significances.

A Journey Through the Infernal Realms

As you turn these pages and meet each of the twenty-four infernal beings, you are invited to delve into their stories, to understand their powers and the symbolism behind their forms. Whether you seek protection, power, wisdom, or simply a profound connection to the mythic, "Infernal Ink" offers a window into the complexities of the shadows that shape our understanding of the light.

In embracing the infernal, you may just find the celestial.

LUCIFER

Lucifer, known as the "Light Bringer" or the "Morning Star," is one of the most compelling figures in Christian and Jewish mythologies. Traditionally seen as the epitome of pride and rebellion, his story is often a tale of ambition, wisdom, and ultimate downfall. Lucifer's narrative is rich with themes of enlightenment and tragic heroism, making him a complex and layered character for artistic exploration.

Symbolic Representation: As the "Light Bringer," Lucifer's imagery often includes motifs of light and fire, not merely to suggest destruction but also illumination—knowledge brought to mankind causing eternal conflict. His torch or the flaming sword that casts out shadows represents the dual nature of enlightenment; it brings warmth and clarity but also pain and disruption.

Cultural Significance: Lucifer's fall from Heaven is emblematic of the ultimate rebellion against divine authority, challenging the cosmos's status quo. This rebellion often mirrors humanity's own struggles against tyranny and the quest for personal autonomy and understanding. In many cultural narratives, Lucifer is not just a villain but a tragic hero who prompts reflection on the nature of sin and redemption.

Artistic Elements: An artistic depiction of Lucifer could emphasize his regal bearing and the stark contrasts in his form—from the divine brightness of his angelic origins to the shadowed, brooding figure he has become. Incorporating elements of classical Renaissance art, such as detailed feather work on the wings and a halo that is broken or tarnished, can symbolize his fall from perfection.

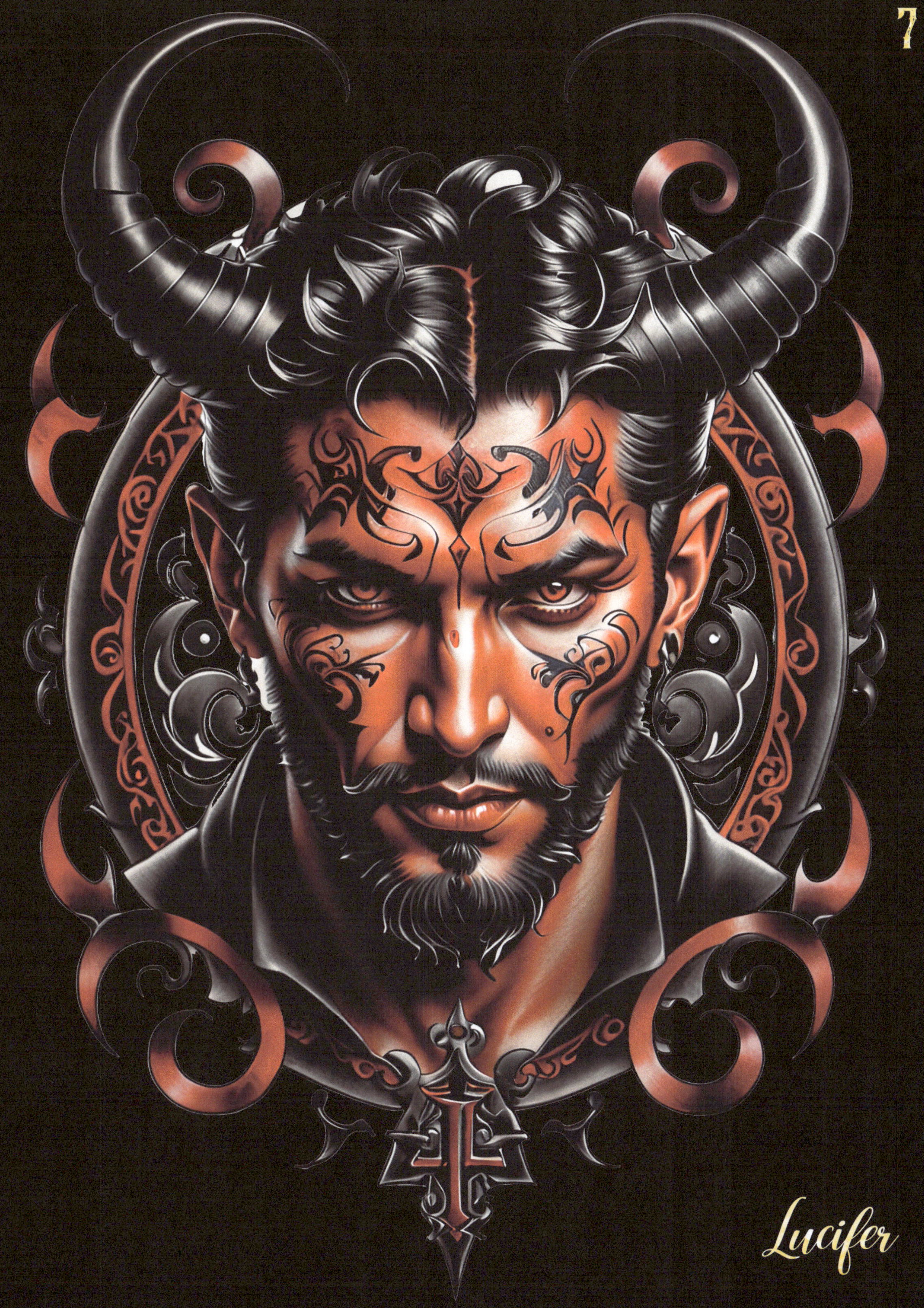
Lucifer

Beelzebub

Beelzebub, also known as the Lord of the Flies, holds a primal and menacing position among the infernal ranks. Traditionally depicted as one of the chief lieutenants of Hell, Beelzebub's name is thought to be derived from the Canaanite god "Baal" and evolved in Abrahamic traditions to embody one of the ultimate forms of filth and corruption.

Symbolic Representation: Beelzebub is a dark mirror to society's excesses—gluttony, waste, and the decay of moral fabric. His presence in art might include scenes where he presides over a banquet of rot, a perverse reflection of societal consumption and the hidden costs it imposes on the environment and the soul. This banquet can be depicted with diners who are oblivious or even enjoying the rotten fare, highlighting ignorance and complicity in societal decay.

Cultural Significance: In the context of Christian demonology, Beelzebub is sometimes considered a high-ranking figure in Satan's army, second only to Lucifer himself. This status as a prince of demons gives him a commanding aura, despite his foul nature. His role involves spreading corruption and facilitating the fall of man through the manipulation of desires—turning basic needs into excessive, destructive wants.

Artistic Elements: For a tattoo design or artistic depiction, highlighting Beelzebub's connection to flies and rot can be impactful. Imagining him with a crown formed of twisted, rusty metal, encrusted with remnants of decay and surrounded by a halo of flies enhances this vision. His eyes, perhaps a sickly yellow, could reflect a cunning intelligence, seeing through societal facades and understanding the true nature of decay.

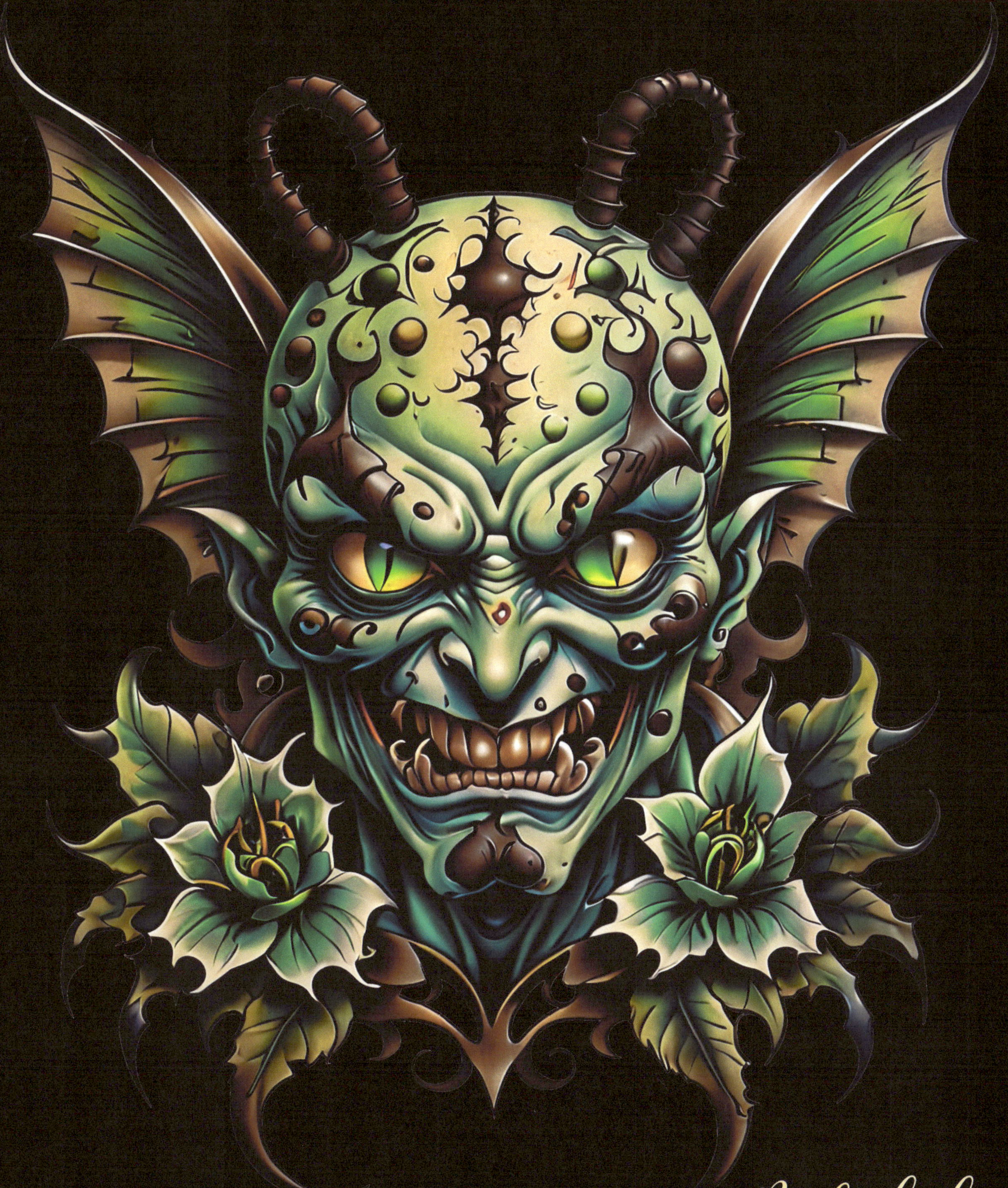

Beelzebub

LEVIATHAN

Leviathan, the twisting sea serpent from biblical lore, is a symbol of primordial chaos and the uncontrollable forces of nature. This monstrous entity is often depicted as a colossal dragon-like creature that resides in the ocean's darkest depths, ruling over all aquatic beings with terrifying supremacy.

Symbolic Representation: Leviathan's imagery is deeply entwined with the forces of chaos that it represents—its very presence distorts the water currents and whirls the sea into frothing tempests. It embodies the destructive power of water, often used as a metaphor for overwhelming emotional or psychological turmoil. The Leviathan can swallow whole ships, just as chaos overwhelms and engulfs order, reflecting the fearsome, consuming nature of the unknown.

Cultural Significance: In various mythologies, Leviathan is sometimes seen as an agent of divine punishment, sent to remind humans of their mortality and insignificance in the face of divine or natural order. Its battles with gods or heroes symbolize the struggle between man and nature, order and chaos, highlighting humanity's perseverance in the face of overwhelming odds.

Artistic Elements: Artistically, Leviathan can be rendered with dramatic contrasts between the deep blues and blacks of the oceanic abyss and the stark, luminous whites and silvers of its eyes and teeth, emphasizing its dual role as a creature of beauty and terror. The dynamic swirling of water around its massive form can be used to convey movement and power, with crashing waves and torn ships to illustrate its destructive capabilities.

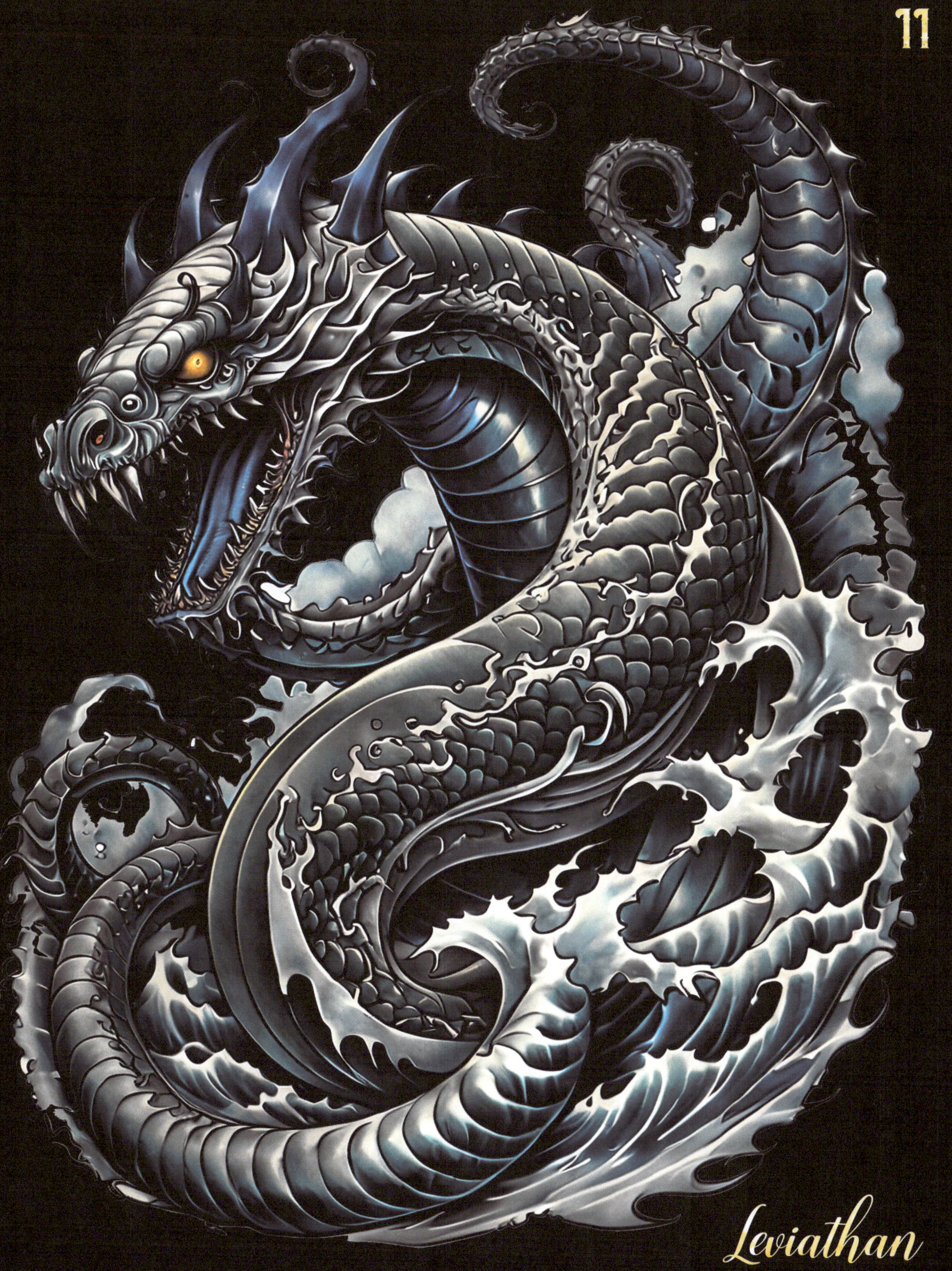

Leviathan

Baal

Baal, one of the most ancient and formidable kings of Hell, is often depicted in grimoires and mythological texts as a demon of fertility and agriculture before his fall. His dominion over the earth and its creatures showcases a juxtaposition of nurturing and predatory instincts, making him a complex figure in demonic lore.

Symbolic Representation: The tri-headed figure of Baal is not just a symbol of his power over the physical realms but also represents the triadic concepts found in many religions and esoteric traditions — such as creation, preservation, and destruction. Baal's presence in art and literature often brings themes of the earth's fertility juxtaposed with the barrenness of deserts and wastelands, illustrating the dual nature of creation and decay. Each head, with its unique sensory perceptions, highlights his omnipresence and omnipotence within his domains.

Cultural Significance: Baal's origins can be traced back to pre-Christian deities associated with nature and agricultural bounty. As a demon, these attributes transformed into a more sinister depiction, representing the overgrowth of natural forces that can both sustain and destroy life. His adaptation into Christian demonology as a Prince of Hell reflects historical shifts in the perception of pagan gods, turning a once-revered deity into a symbol of paganism's suppression.

Artistic Elements: In artistic depictions, Baal can be envisioned seated on a throne of roots and vines that spread across the ground, entwining the bones of past sacrifices — a stark reminder of his rule over life and death. His eyes could be illustrated as deeply luminous, reflecting the earth's verdant colors, while his voice, though raucous, carries the compelling power of the wild, commanding the spirits of the earth.

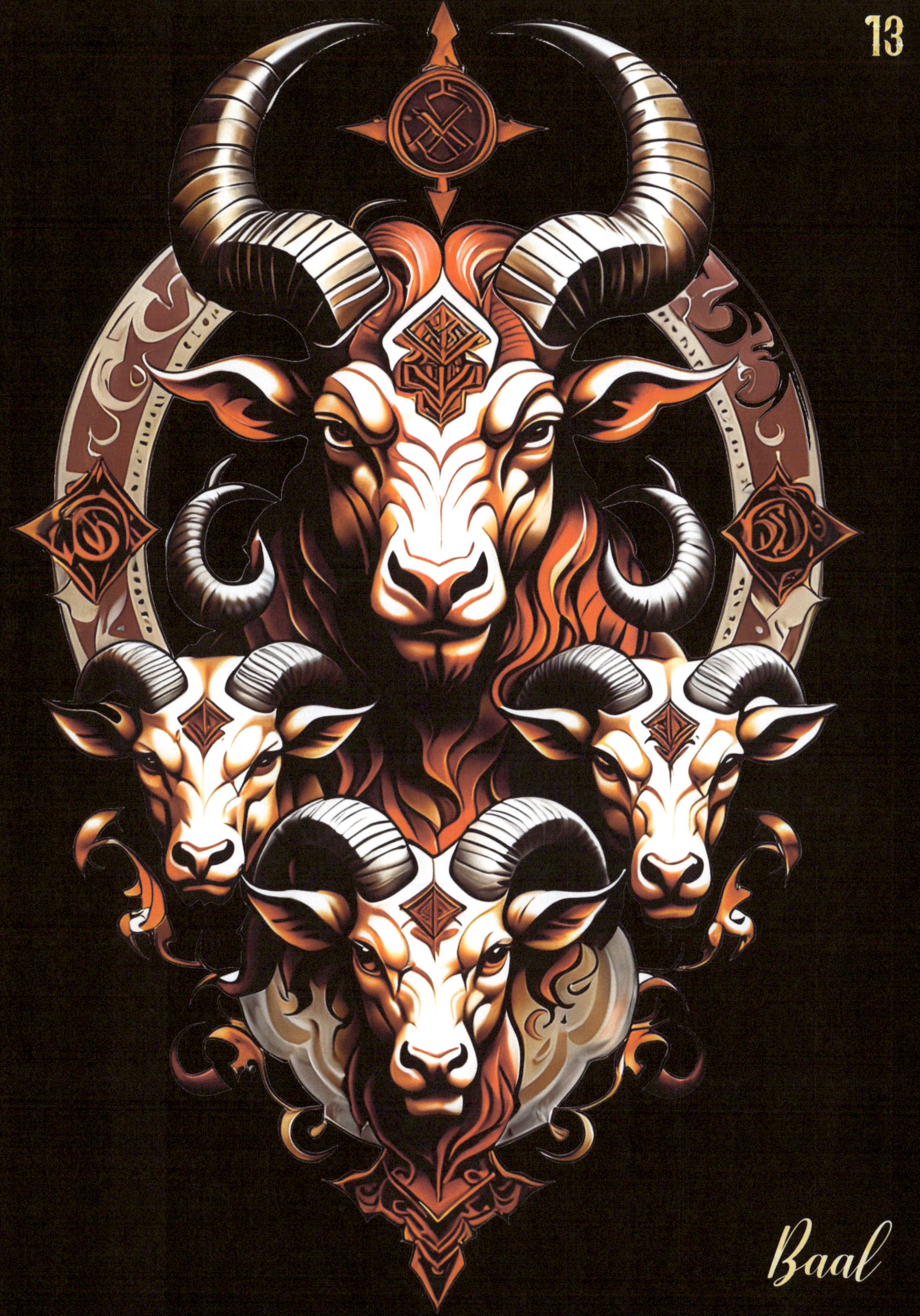

Baal

Asmodeus

Asmodeus, also known as Asmodai, is a demon primarily associated with lust and manipulation, heralding from ancient Judaic lore where he appears as a king of demons and an antagonist to human happiness. His dominion over human desires makes him a compelling figure in mythological studies, often portrayed as the embodiment of lust and the arbiter of seduction.

Symbolic Representation: He often holds a heart pierced by arrows, a direct symbol of the painful aspects of love and the dualities of human emotion — attraction intertwined with danger and satisfaction mingled with despair. This imagery reflects Asmodeus's role not only as a promoter of physical desire but also as a manipulator of the heart's more metaphysical afflictions, embodying the complexities of human relationships and the often destructive nature of unchecked passion.

Cultural Significance: Asmodeus's roots can be traced back to Persian and Near Eastern mythologies, where he was seen as a demon of wrath and revenge. Over time, his legend evolved in the Judaic and Christian traditions to highlight themes of lust and seduction, portraying him as a destroyer of matrimonial fidelity and a corrupter of innocence. This transformation in his mythological role reflects broader cultural anxieties about morality, sin, and the dangers of temptation.

Artistic Elements: Artistically, Asmodeus can be rendered surrounded by motifs of decadence and decay, such as a throne adorned with vanitas symbols like wilting flowers and rotting fruits, which underscore the transient pleasure and ultimate dissatisfaction that carnal desires often bring. His attire, richly detailed and colored in dark, passionate hues—deep reds and shadowy blacks—can further emphasize his dominion over the darker side of love.

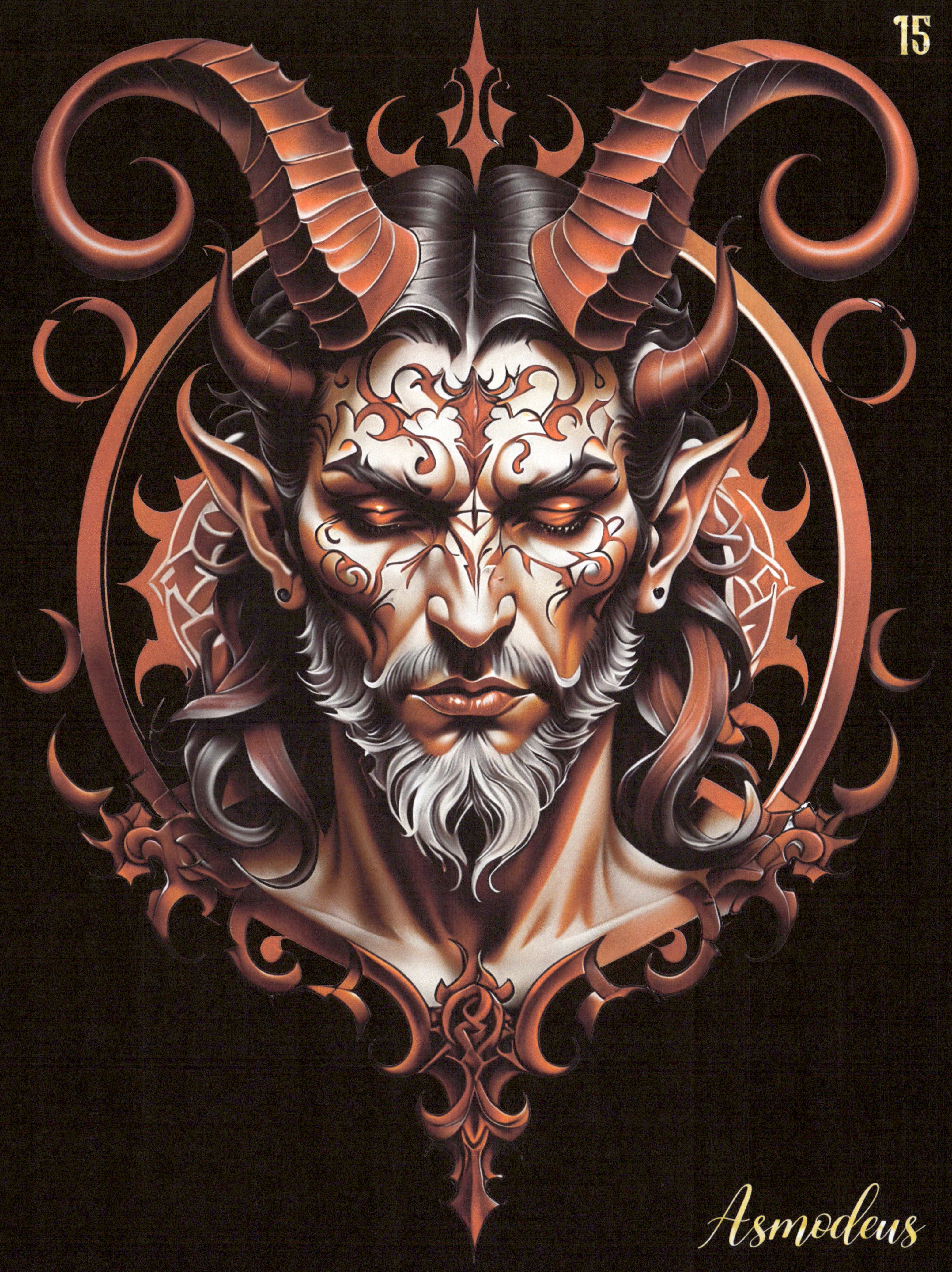

Asmodeus

ABADDON

Abaddon, often referred to as the "Destroyer" in biblical texts, holds a fearsome reputation as the overseer of the abyss and a harbinger of the apocalypse. His name, derived from a Hebrew word meaning "destruction," perfectly encapsulates his role within mythological traditions as an angel or demon presiding over ultimate ruin and the purgation of sin.

Symbolic Representation: The imagery of locusts serves to underscore Abaddon's role as a divine executioner, sent to purge the world of its sins through destructive, yet ultimately purifying, wrath. His presence often coincides with the sounding of trumpets that herald the end times, as described in Revelations, where he leads an army of locusts to enact judgment upon the earth.

Cultural Significance: In cultural and theological contexts, Abaddon represents the inevitable force of decay and destruction that all civilizations must reckon with. He embodies the concept that from destruction comes rebirth, a necessary end that precedes any new beginning. His dual nature as both angel and demon in various texts reflects the complex interplay between divine retribution and satanic ruin.

Artistic Elements: Artistically, Abaddon can be rendered amidst scenes of apocalyptic desolation—cities in ruin, landscapes barren and blighted, skies darkened by swarms of his locusts. His figure, while central, might also be somewhat obscured by the chaos surrounding him, highlighting his role as the impersonal force of destruction rather than a personal antagonist. His eyes, if visible, could glow with the fire of righteous fury, a stark contrast to the cool, emotionless metal of his armor

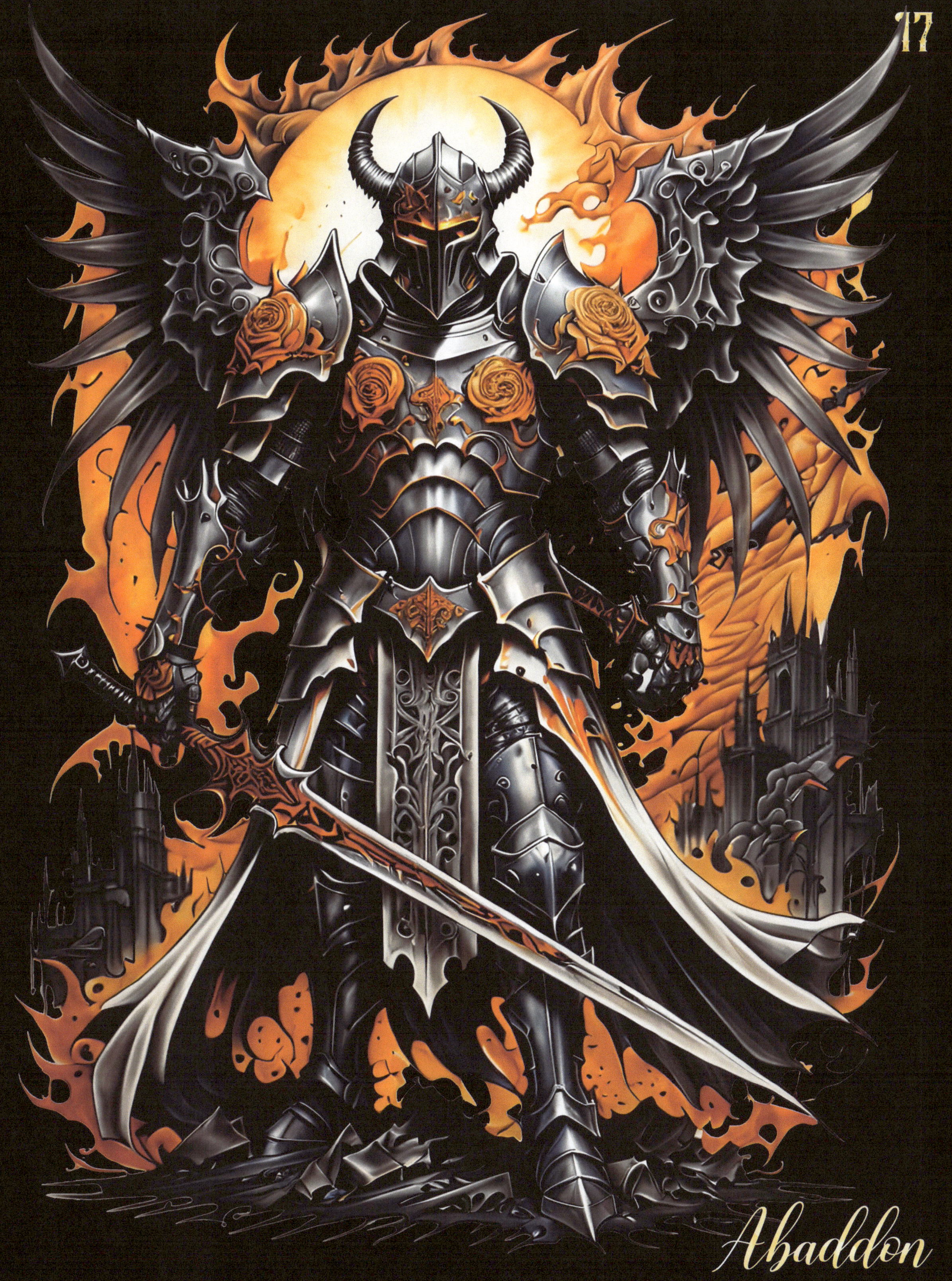

Abaddon

Mammon

Mammon is traditionally recognized in Christian theology as the demon of greed, avarice, and excess. His name itself has become synonymous with wealth and materialism, often cited as an entity that seduces through the allure of riches. Mammon's portrayal as a corpulent demon eloquently symbolizes the excess and corruption that follow the unrestrained pursuit of material wealth.

Symbolic Representation: The image of Mammon is not just a literal depiction of greed but also a metaphor for the spiritual bankruptcy that accompanies the blind pursuit of material gain. The chains of gold that bind him—and those he ensnares—serve as powerful symbols of addiction and enslavement to wealth. His throne, while opulent, is also a cage, illustrating that the pursuit of material excess traps the seeker as much as it rewards him.

Cultural Significance: Mammon embodies the dark side of material success and the moral and ethical dilemmas associated with it. His figure serves as a cautionary tale against the idolatry of money, highlighting how wealth can corrupt and degrade human values if left unchecked. This demon's lore encourages reflection on the true cost of wealth and the sacrifices made in its pursuit.

Artistic Elements: In artistic depictions, Mammon can be surrounded by symbols of commerce and finance—scales, coins, ledgers filled with endless entries, all tarnished or corrupted in some way. His domain might be envisioned as a cavernous treasury that resembles a mausoleum, filled with the accumulated wealth of ages but devoid of life or joy. The color palette could include golds and yellows juxtaposed with dark shadows, emphasizing the stark contrasts between wealth and the darkness it can bring.

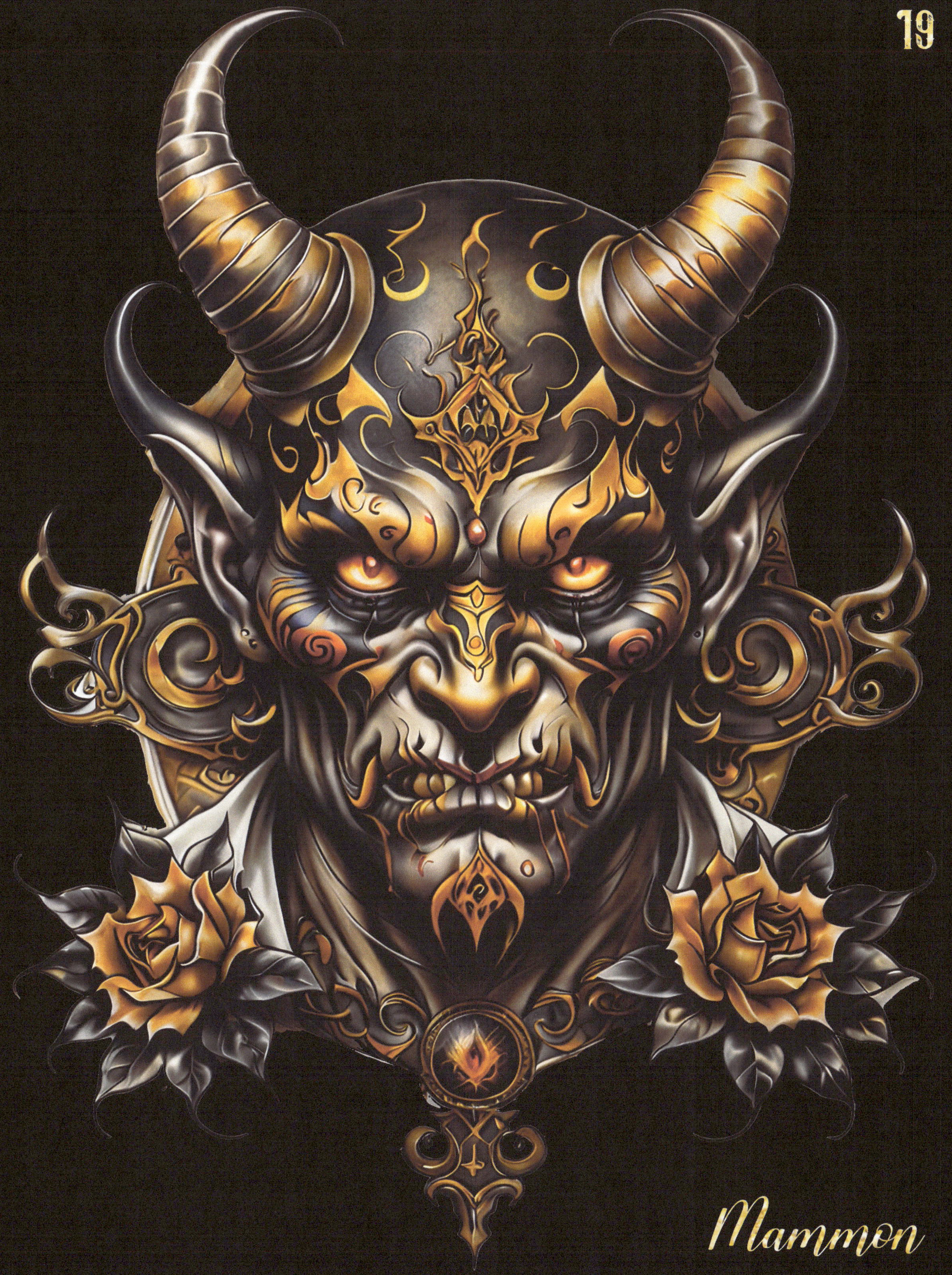
Mammon

Belphegor

Belphegor, a demon whose origins may trace back to Moabite mythology as a god of abundance and fertility, has evolved in Christian demonology into a symbol of inventiveness and indolence. This paradoxical figure is associated with both the ingenious breakthroughs that drive societies forward and the sloth and decadence that can result from such progress.

Symbolic Representation: Often seated upon a throne that mimics an ergonomic office chair, Belphegor holds a Macbook or similar device, through which he disseminates his brilliant yet ensnaring ideas. The screen glows with enticing projects and endless distractions, pulling in all who gaze upon it and binding them with the golden chains of procrastination and idle pleasure. This imagery not only highlights his domain over sloth but also his governance of the creative sparks that lead to technological advancements and ultimately, cultural decay.

Cultural Significance: Belphegor's dual nature reflects modern societal concerns regarding technology and progress. He personifies the struggle between benefiting from new inventions and becoming overly dependent on them, thus losing vital skills and work ethics. His lore prompts a reflection on the balance between innovation and the potential moral and spiritual cost of such developments.

Artistic Elements: Artistically, Belphegor can be rendered with a backdrop of half-finished projects and innovative but unused tools, cluttered around his throne like trophies. These items, detailed and modern, contrast starkly with the ancient, rune-inscribed walls of his lair—suggesting a disconnect between past wisdom and modern practices. The lighting in his domain is dim, punctuated only by the harsh artificial light from screens, casting long shadows and creating an atmosphere of stagnation and forgotten priorities.

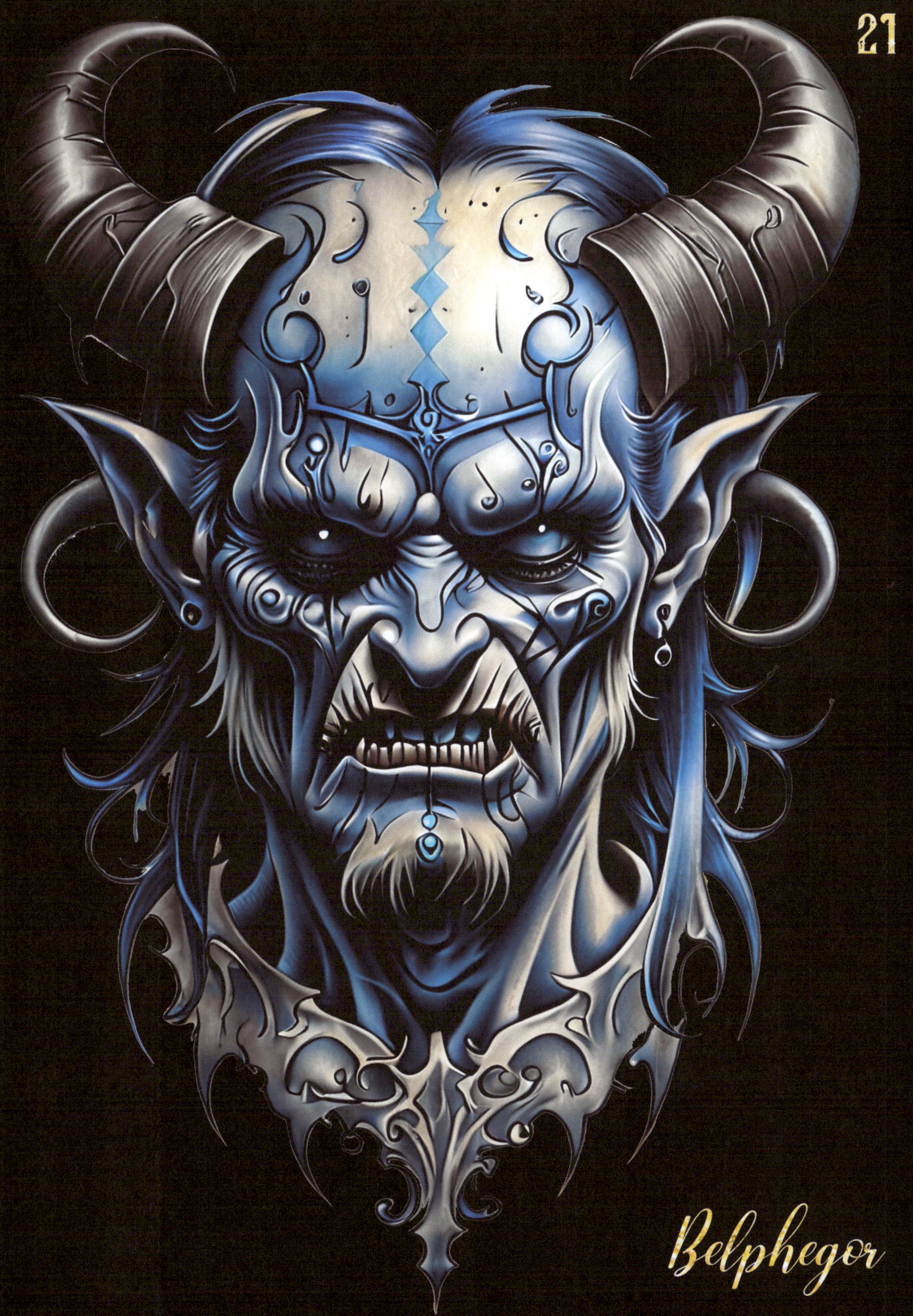

Belphegor

Samael

Samael, often termed the Angel of Death in various mythological traditions, embodies the paradoxical nature of mortality. His presence is feared as the harbinger of the end, yet he also represents transformation and the essential passage to renewal. As a complex figure, Samael bridges the worlds of life and death, serving as a reminder of the inevitability and impartiality of the ultimate fate that awaits all living beings.

Symbolic Representation: In his hands, Samael often carries a scythe or a sword, traditional symbols of the Angel of Death, which he uses to cut down the threads of life. This imagery emphasizes his role as an executor of divine will, a necessary force that maintains the balance of the universe by ensuring the end of life cycles. His eyes, if visible, might glow with a somber, wise light, reflecting the depth of knowledge that only one who has seen countless eons pass could possess.

Cultural Significance: Samael's depiction as both an angelic figure and a demonic entity in different cultures highlights the dual aspects of death—feared and avoided, yet also accepted as a natural and essential part of existence. He embodies the mysterious and often taboo nature of death in human society, serving as a cultural touchstone for discussions about mortality, the afterlife, and the moral implications of life-ending actions.

Artistic Elements: Artistically, Samael can be rendered standing at the threshold of worlds; perhaps a gate or a doorway that divides the living from the dead. This gate could be adorned with symbols of life—flowers, vibrant colors, images of the sun—and symbols of death—skulls, wilting flowers, moons. The contrast in this imagery serves to highlight the transitions Samael oversees. His figure, though cloaked in darkness, might be outlined with an ethereal glow, suggesting his divine nature and the solemn dignity of his duty.

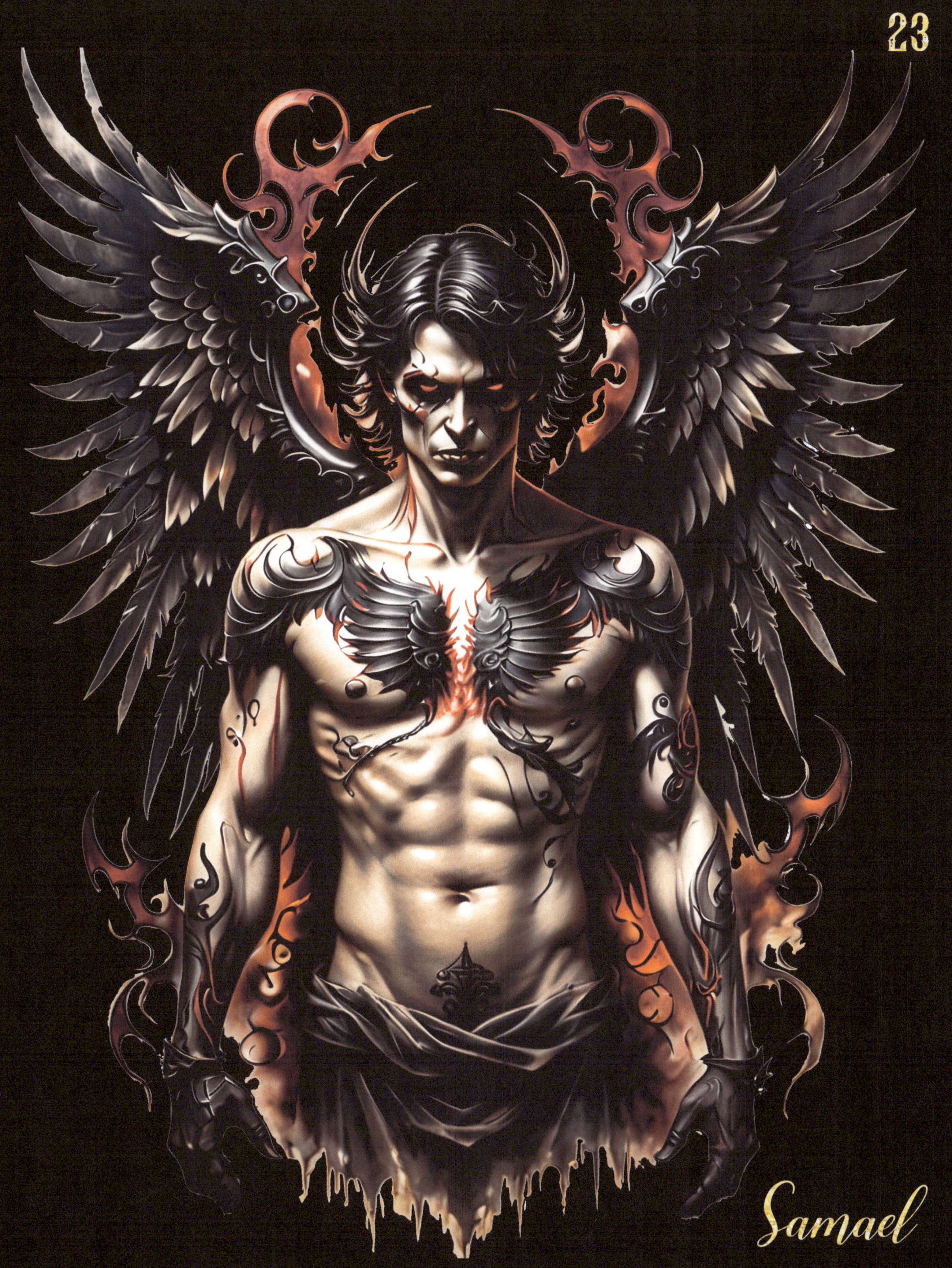

Samael

Lilith

Lilith, often regarded as the first woman in ancient mythologies, embodies dark independence and the untamed aspects of nature. She is a figure wrapped in the shadows of legend, known for her defiance and as a symbol of feminine power. Lilith's narrative is steeped in themes of rebellion against subservience and the exploration of the more profound, often darker, aspects of freedom and equality.

Symbolic Representation: Her silhouette is often surrounded by motifs of the moon and nocturnal creatures, emphasizing her role as a guardian of secrets and mysteries. Lilith's presence in art can be surrounded by symbols of fertility and desolation alike, representing her complex nature as both a creator and a destroyer, a giver of life and a bringer of death. Her imagery often includes serpents or owls, creatures that in many cultures symbolize wisdom and death, further highlighting her dual roles.

Cultural Significance: In cultural narratives, Lilith is seen as a figure who challenges the traditional roles assigned to women, embodying the raw, unbound aspects of feminine essence. Her story resonates with themes of independence, equality, and justice, often making her a symbol for those who stand against the oppressive structures of society. Lilith's tale invites reflection on the nature of freedom and the societal chains that bind spirits and bodies.

Artistic Elements: Artistically, Lilith can be rendered in environments that symbolize both the beauty and isolation of her legend. She might be placed in a lush, forbidden garden at twilight, representing the Garden of Eden from which she is said to have been exiled, or perched atop craggy cliffs overlooking stormy seas, symbolizing her dominion over chaos and untamed nature. The use of deep blues, purples, and blacks in her portrayal can emphasize her nocturnal and mysterious attributes.

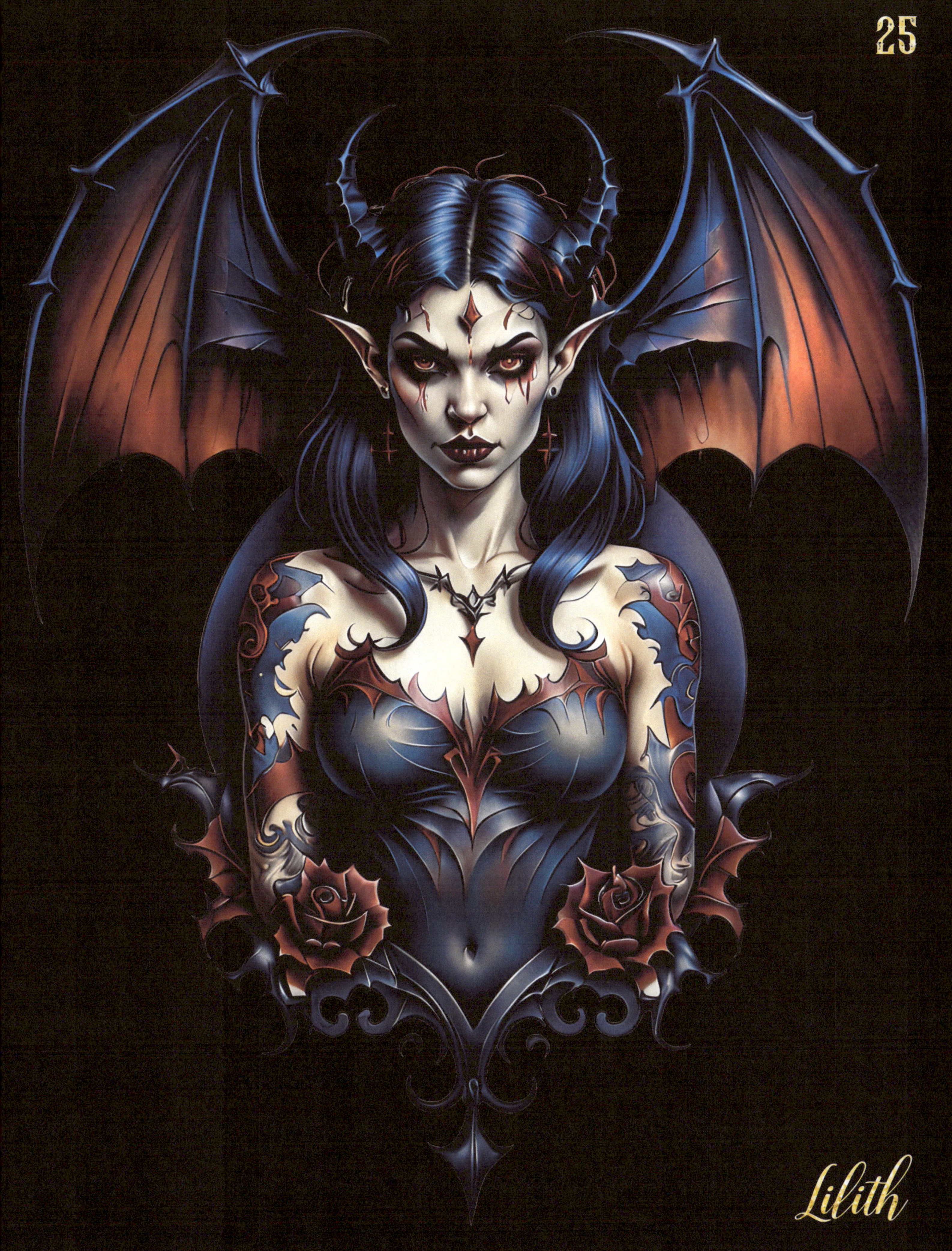

Lilith

Astaroth

Astaroth, a Duke of Hell in demonological traditions, stands as a symbol of intellectual persuasion and forbidden wisdom. Historically revered and feared for his deep knowledge of the past, as well as his ability to uncover hidden secrets, Astaroth navigates the complexities of time and memory, often serving as a grand librarian of infernal archives. His role transcends mere temptation, delving into the seduction of the intellect with truths that mortals might find both compelling and overwhelming.

Symbolic Representation: The imagery of Astaroth is rife with symbols of enlightenment and peril. The serpent and the book represent dual avenues of knowledge—the intuitive and the learned, each with its own dangers and allure. His surroundings, adorned with infernal symbols, underscore his authority over hidden knowledge and the forbidden arts. These symbols often include esoteric sigils that promise power but also portend doom.

Cultural Significance: Astaroth's lore integrates elements of ancient deities associated with wisdom and the underworld, often drawing parallels with figures like Ishtar and Asherah. In medieval and Renaissance occultism, Astaroth was invoked for his ability to grant wisdom and to teach artistic skills, reflecting the human yearning for divine insight and the perilous bargains that often accompany such quests.

Artistic Elements: In artistic portrayals, Astaroth could be envisioned within a grand, shadowy library of Hell, where the shelves are endless and the books are bound in strange leathers. The atmosphere is thick with the musk of moldy tomes and the crackle of burning paper, reflecting the perpetual decay and renewal of knowledge. His eyes might glow with a scholar's fervor, casting an eerie, sage light that beckons the viewer closer, tempting them with the secrets of the ages.

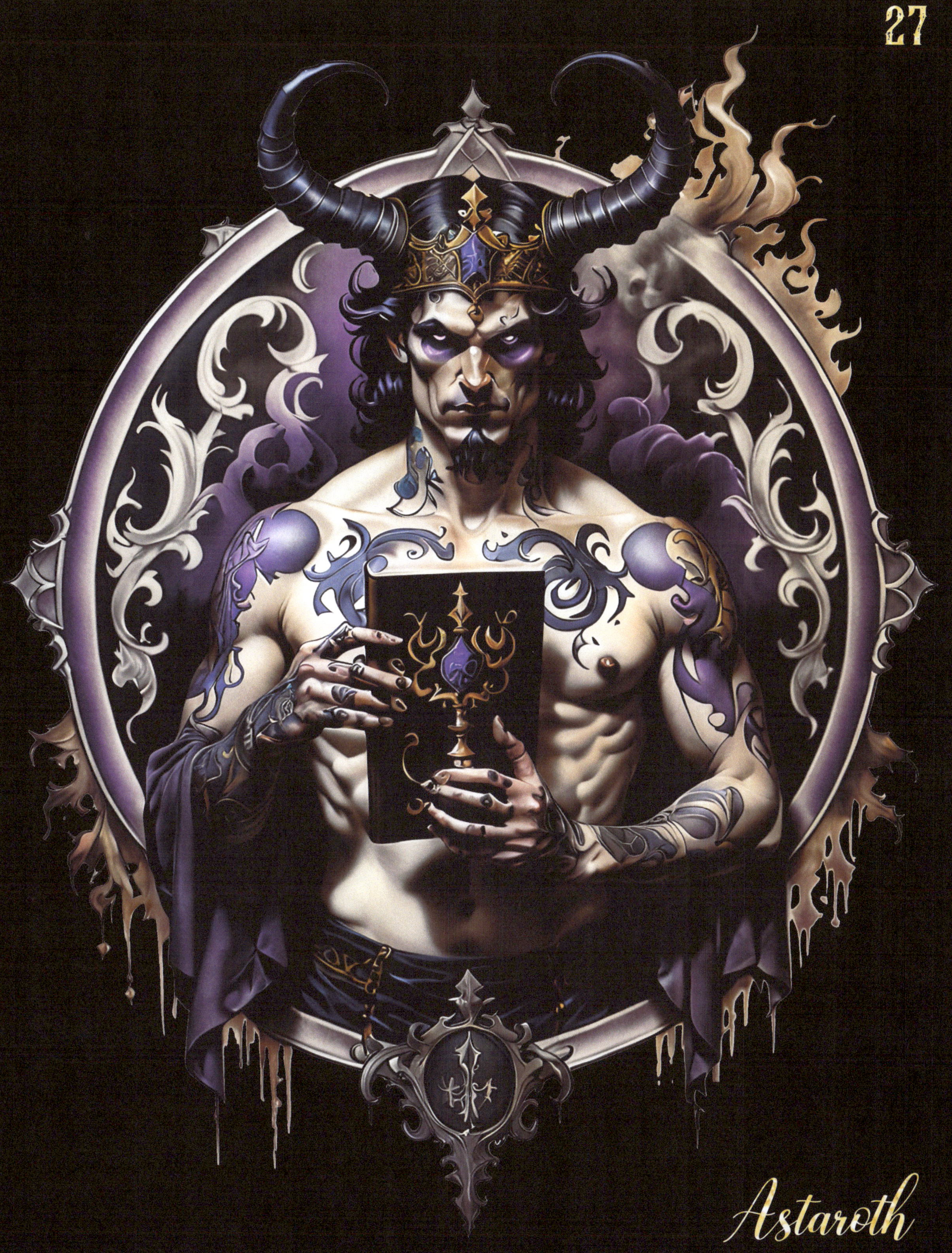

Astaroth

Belial

Belial, a name derived from the Hebrew word for "without value" or "wickedness," is often depicted in texts as the personification of lawlessness and the epitome of dissension. He is characterized as a figure who rejects all hierarchical and societal norms, positioned as a demonic leader who incites rebellion and thrives in the chaos that ensues. Belial's defiance is not just against divine order but against all forms of governance that suppress freedom and autonomy.

Symbolic Representation: Belial's presence amidst flames underscores his role as an instigator of upheaval; fire symbolizes both destruction and purification, reflecting his aim to dismantle corrupt systems to forge something anew from the ashes. His hands might be raised in a gesture of domination and defiance, rallying the dispossessed and the disenfranchised who gather at his call. The chains that once might have bound him lie broken at his feet, symbolizing his release from the shackles of divine and mortal rule.

Cultural Significance: Historically, Belial has been depicted as a demon of deceit and guilt, a corrupter who tempts humans to break moral and societal laws. In modern interpretations, he can be seen as a radical antihero, challenging oppressive structures and advocating for a reevaluation of moral and ethical boundaries. His narrative invites discussions about the nature of freedom versus anarchy and the complex dance between societal order and personal liberty.

Artistic Elements: Artistically, Belial can be rendered in environments that are chaotic yet transformative—burnt-out ruins of what once was, with new life emerging among the ashes, symbolizing the potential for renewal post-revolution. His figure could be juxtaposed against a backdrop of stark, apocalyptic beauty—cities on the verge of collapse, skies alight with the glow of fire, all conveying the destructive yet cleansing power of his influence.

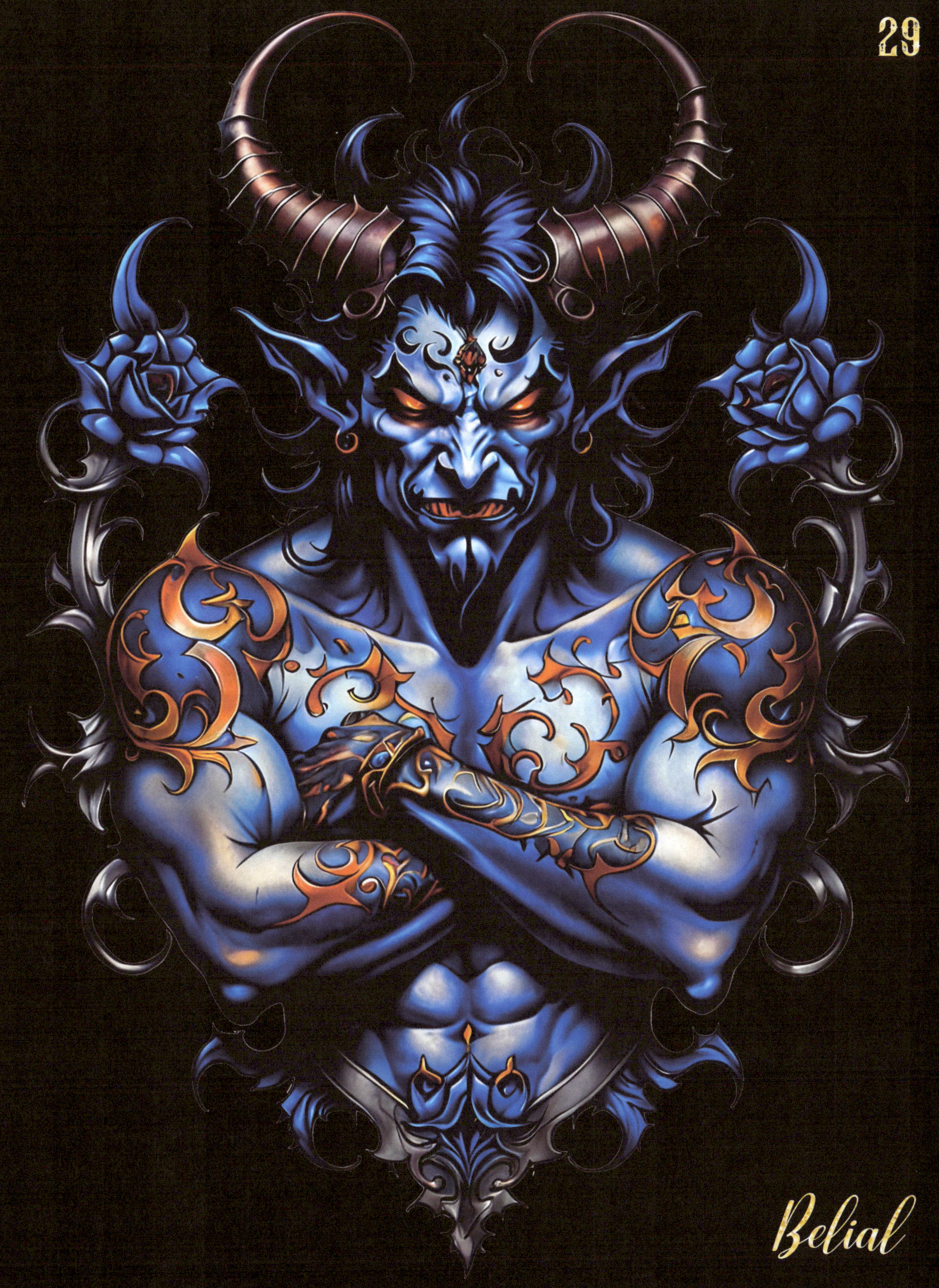

Belial

Pazuzu

Pazuzu is an ancient Mesopotamian demon of the wind, known both for his fearsome destructive power and his unexpected protective instincts. This demon embodies the duality of nature's force—both creator and destroyer, he brings life-giving rains and also devastating storms. His image has historically been invoked both for protection against malevolent spirits and as a symbol of terror.

Symbolic Representation: Pazuzu is often depicted with a scowling visage and outstretched wings that dominate the skies, a figure meant to inspire fear and awe. This fearsome appearance serves a dual purpose—it wards off evil spirits, harnessing his terrifying image to protect those who invoke his name. The expansive wings symbolize his control over the vast domain of the air, capable of summoning hurricanes and tempests that reshape landscapes and destinies. His growling demeanor and twisted features also reflect the chaotic and unpredictable nature of the winds he commands.

Cultural Significance: In ancient Mesopotamian culture, Pazuzu was a complex figure, sometimes seen as a malevolent demon but also respected as a protector against plagues and evils. His statues and amulets were used as talismans to protect against the forces of destruction and illness, particularly to safeguard pregnant women and children. This protective aspect highlights a broader cultural understanding of the elemental forces as entities that required both reverence and caution.

Artistic Elements: Without focusing solely on the visual, the artistic portrayal of Pazuzu could integrate elements that symbolize his dual nature. For instance, narratives or artworks might depict scenes where his intervention via the winds saves a crop from drought, but the same winds later bring a storm that causes a flood. Such depictions highlight his capricious nature and the ancient human attempt to understand and negotiate with the elemental powers

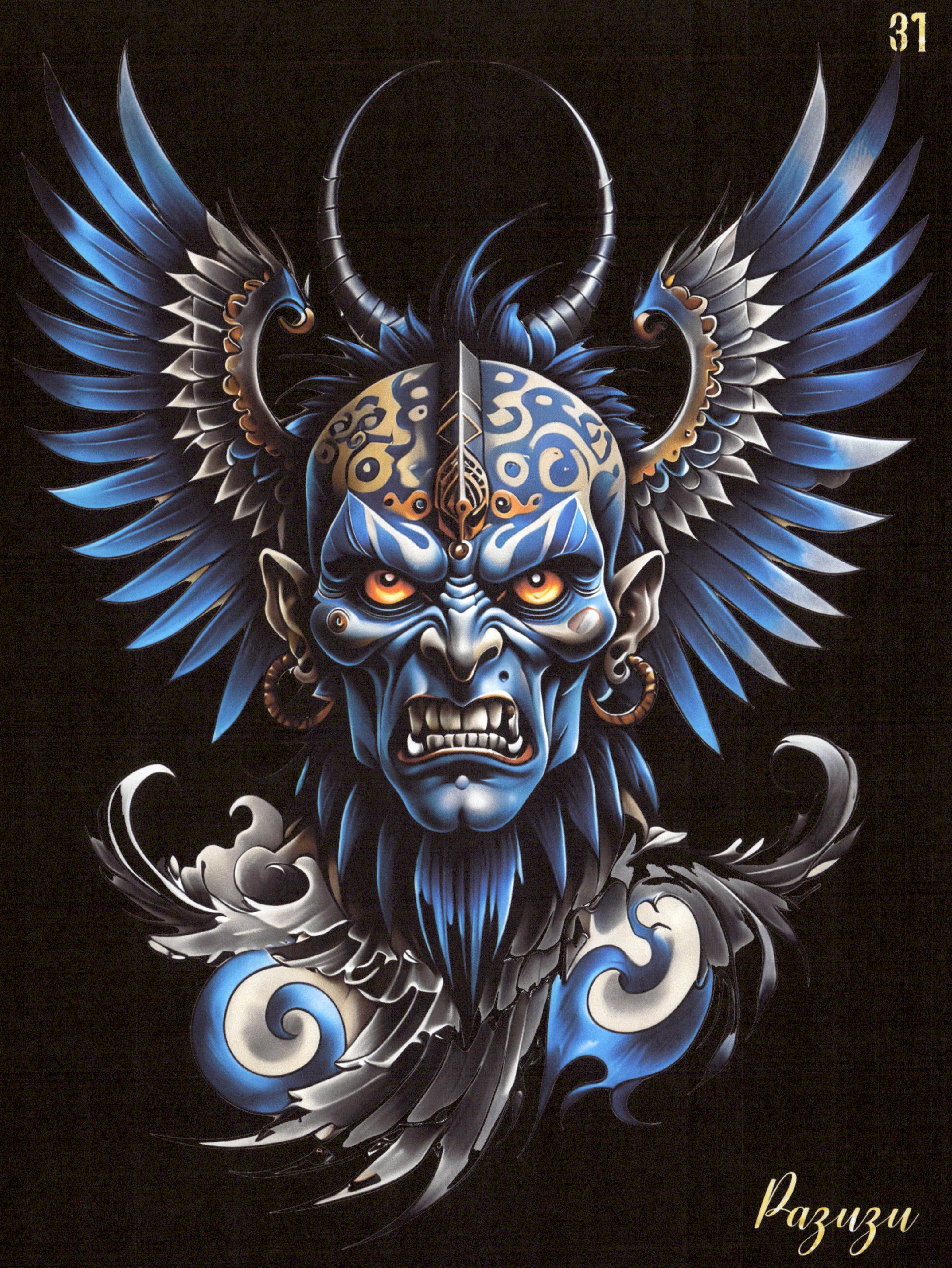

Pazuzu

Baphomet

Baphomet is a figure shrouded in mystery and controversy, often associated with the esoteric and the occult. Originating possibly from misinterpretations of the name "Mahomet" (Muhammad) during the Crusades, Baphomet has evolved in modern times into a symbol of the synthesis of opposites, a complex icon representing the duality of existence. This enigmatic idol is not merely a deity of chaos or order, but a profound embodiment of their union and balance.

Symbolic Representation: Baphomet is typically depicted as a hermaphroditic figure with a goat's head, symbolizing fertility, instinct, and the earth, coupled with human body features that represent intellect and the higher spiritual planes. This dual-gender nature highlights the theme of balance between male and female energies, essential for the mystic harmony the figure is said to represent. The torch between its horns casts light upon the hidden truths of the universe and the path to enlightenment, guiding the followers through the darkness of ignorance and superstition.

Cultural Significance: Baphomet's image has been adopted by numerous esoteric traditions, including the Templars according to popular myths, and later the Knights of the Order of the Temple in the 19th century, and more contemporarily by certain modern occult groups. Each iteration has viewed Baphomet as a complex symbol of opposing forces: good and evil, male and female, above and below. This figure challenges the viewer to acknowledge the complexity of reality and the necessity of embracing all aspects of life to find true enlightenment.

Artistic Elements: The artistic portrayal of Baphomet might emphasize the unity of opposites through additional symbolic imagery: the moon and the sun, water and fire, earth and air—all orchestrated around him in a harmonious tableau that invites contemplation. His posture, serene yet imposing, suggests both receptivity and authority, inviting onlookers to learn but also to respect the mysteries he guards.

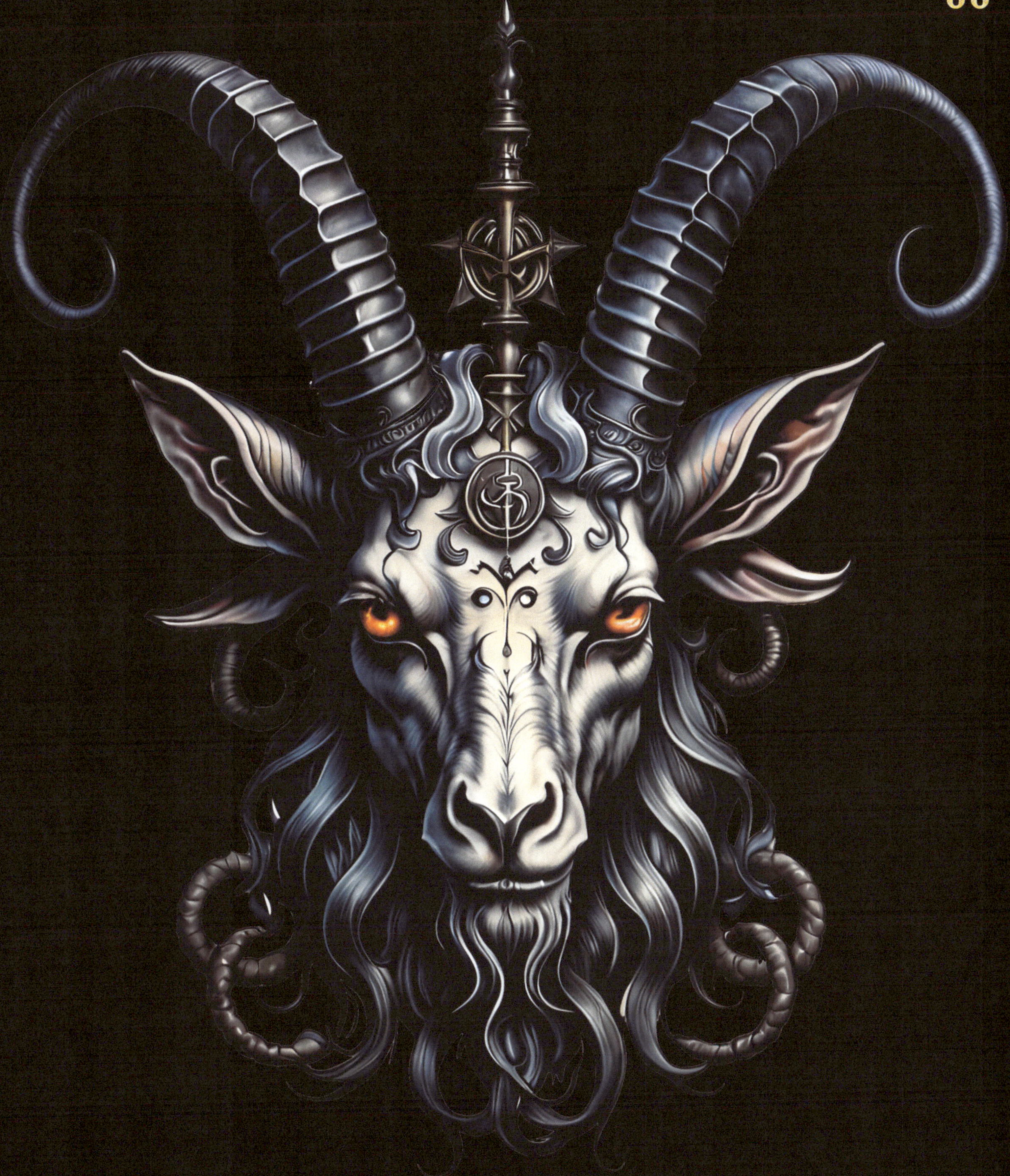

Baphomet

Vine

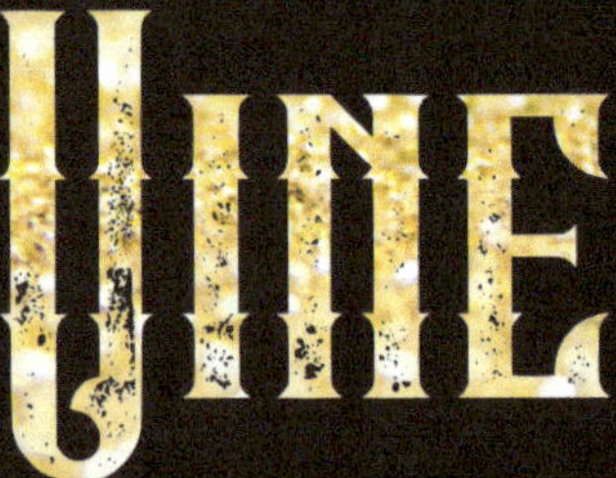

Vine is a demon counted among the nobility of Hell, specifically known for his command over the elements of wood and nature. He is a figure that personifies the primal and untamed aspects of the natural world, depicted with the head of a lion and the tail of a serpent, embodying strength, sovereignty, and cunning. His control over trees and plants symbolizes a deep, intrinsic connection to the earth, positioned uniquely at the intersection of growth and decay.

Symbolic Representation: Vine's imagery as a lion with a serpent's tail coiled around a crumbling column offers a rich tapestry of symbolic meanings. The lion, king of beasts, represents dominion and raw power, while the serpent is a creature of renewal and cunning, symbolizing transformation and healing. This combination underscores Vine's dual ability to nurture and destroy, reflecting the cyclic nature of the natural world. The column, a symbol of human achievement and stability, now in ruins, highlights his role in demonstrating the impermanence of human constructs in the face of nature's enduring and overpowering presence.

Cultural Significance: Vine's portrayal taps into a deep vein of mythological symbolism where nature deities are often depicted as embodying both protective and destructive aspects. In many cultures, such entities serve as reminders of humanity's vulnerability to the earth's raw forces and the respect and reverence this commands. Vine's dominion over wood and nature positions him as a guardian of the wild, commanding the earth to quake and roots to bind, often interpreted as a metaphor for the environmental impacts of neglecting natural harmony.

Artistic Elements: Artistically, Vine can be visualized in a setting that is both lush and menacing—a forest where the trees are alive, their branches twisting in impossible, often eerie shapes, embodying his command over them. The crumbling column, overgrown with ivy and moss, stands as a testament to the relentless power of nature as it reclaims the constructs of civilization. This scene not only captures the essence of Vine's powers but also provides a visually striking metaphor for the interaction between the cultivated and the wild, the tamed and the untamable.

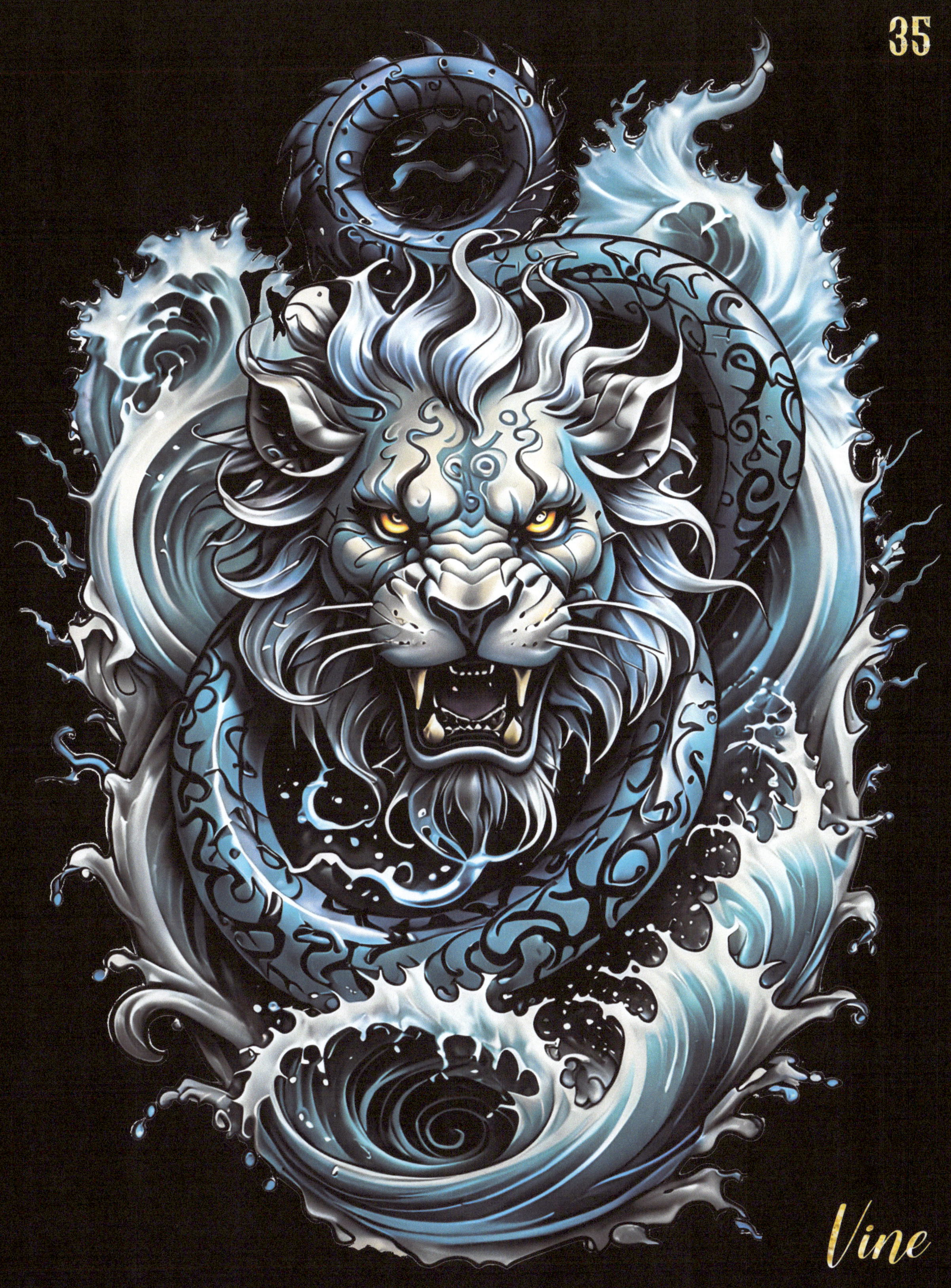
Vine

Andras

Andras is a demon known in demonic lore as the inciter of discord and the orchestrator of conflicts. He is often depicted as a fearsome figure with the head of an owl, symbolizing wisdom used for malevolent purposes, and a body clad in battle armor, indicating his readiness to engage in and propagate strife. His attributes exemplify the destructive aspects of conflicts, particularly those born from misunderstandings or malevolent intentions.

Symbolic Representation: Andras' portrayal with an owl's head atop a warrior's body is a potent symbol of the misuse of intelligence and strategic thinking for destructive ends. The owl, typically a symbol of wisdom, here takes on a darker aspect, representing knowledge twisted for chaos and conflict. His drawn sword not only reinforces his role as a combatant but also symbolizes the sharp, cutting nature of conflict—quick to erupt and deadly in its consequences. This imagery highlights the dual nature of intellect and power, serving as a cautionary tale about the potential fallout when such attributes are directed toward discord.

Cultural Significance: In many cultures, owls are seen as omens of death or harbingers of misfortune, which complements Andras' role in leading men to battle. His presence in mythological narratives often serves as a reminder of the perils of unchecked aggression and the ease with which peace can be shattered by incitement. Andras embodies the chaotic elements of human nature, illustrating the fine line between using one's capabilities for leadership and manipulation, and the consequences of tipping this balance towards anarchy.

Artistic Elements: Artistically, Andras can be depicted in a tumultuous battlefield environment, where the chaos of war is in full display—smoke and fire billowing, soldiers clashing, and the desolate aftermath of such conflicts. His figure, central amidst this chaos, serves as a stark focal point, drawing the eye with the ominous glow of his owl eyes, which could be portrayed as eerily luminous amidst the surrounding darkness. The background might include torn banners and broken weapons, symbolizing the futility and destruction wrought by senseless wars.

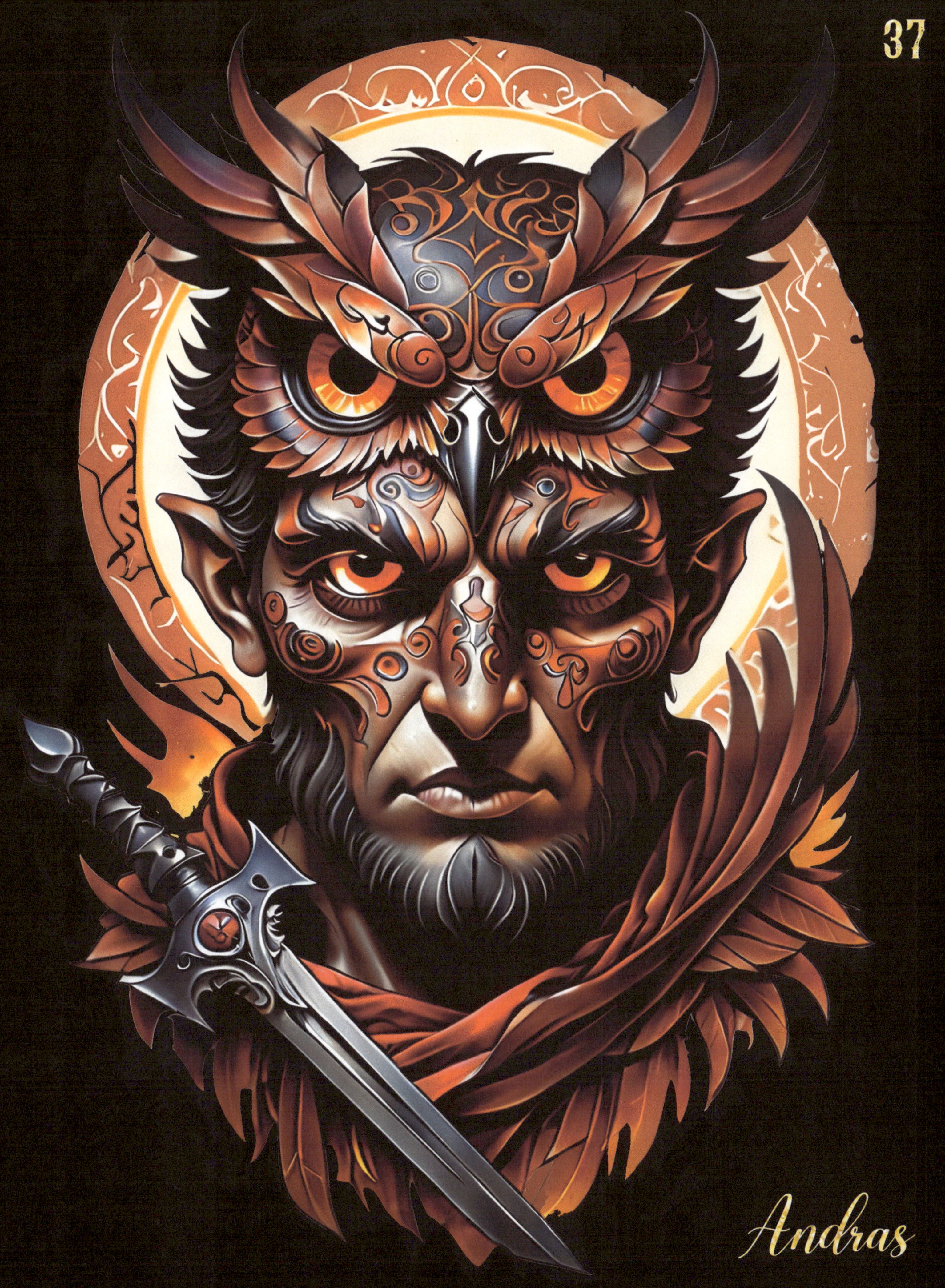
Andras

Furfur

Furfur, a demon of the tempest, commands the fearsome elements of thunder, lightning, and the deceptive forces that echo the chaotic nature of storms. This entity is not only a harbinger of meteorological upheaval but also a metaphorical figure representing the tumultuous and unpredictable forces within human nature and society. He is often visualized in the form of a majestic stag, an embodiment of the noble yet wild aspects of the natural world, with antlers that crackle with the vibrant energy of an electric storm.

Symbolic Representation: The imagery of Furfur as a stag with glowing, electrically charged antlers powerfully symbolizes his dominion over thunder and lightning—forces that are both destructive and revitalizing. Stags are traditionally seen as regal and untamed creatures, symbolizing purity, renewal, and the inherent wildness of nature. Furfur's glowing form and crackling antlers highlight the dual nature of storms as bearers of life-giving water and unpredictable destructive power. This depiction also hints at the deceptive aspects of his character, mirroring the way storms can suddenly transform from calm to catastrophic.

Cultural Significance: In many cultures, stags are associated with various deities and spirits of nature and fertility, making Furfur's chosen form significant in terms of cultural mythology. His connection to storms—a natural phenomenon feared and revered by ancient and modern societies alike—places him at the heart of human interactions with the divine and the natural. Storms, often seen as expressions of divine displeasure or chaotic disruption, perfectly encapsulate Furfur's role as a manipulator of the physical and metaphysical worlds.

Artistic Elements: Artistically, Furfur can be portrayed in a dramatic, stormy landscape where the skies are a tumultuous canvas of dark, brooding clouds and sporadic flashes of lightning. His ethereal glow and the electric crackle of his antlers can be used to cast eerie, flickering shadows that dance unpredictably, enhancing his mystical and intimidating presence. This atmospheric setting not only underscores his command over storms but also the emotional and psychological impact of his presence—inspiring awe and fear simultaneously.

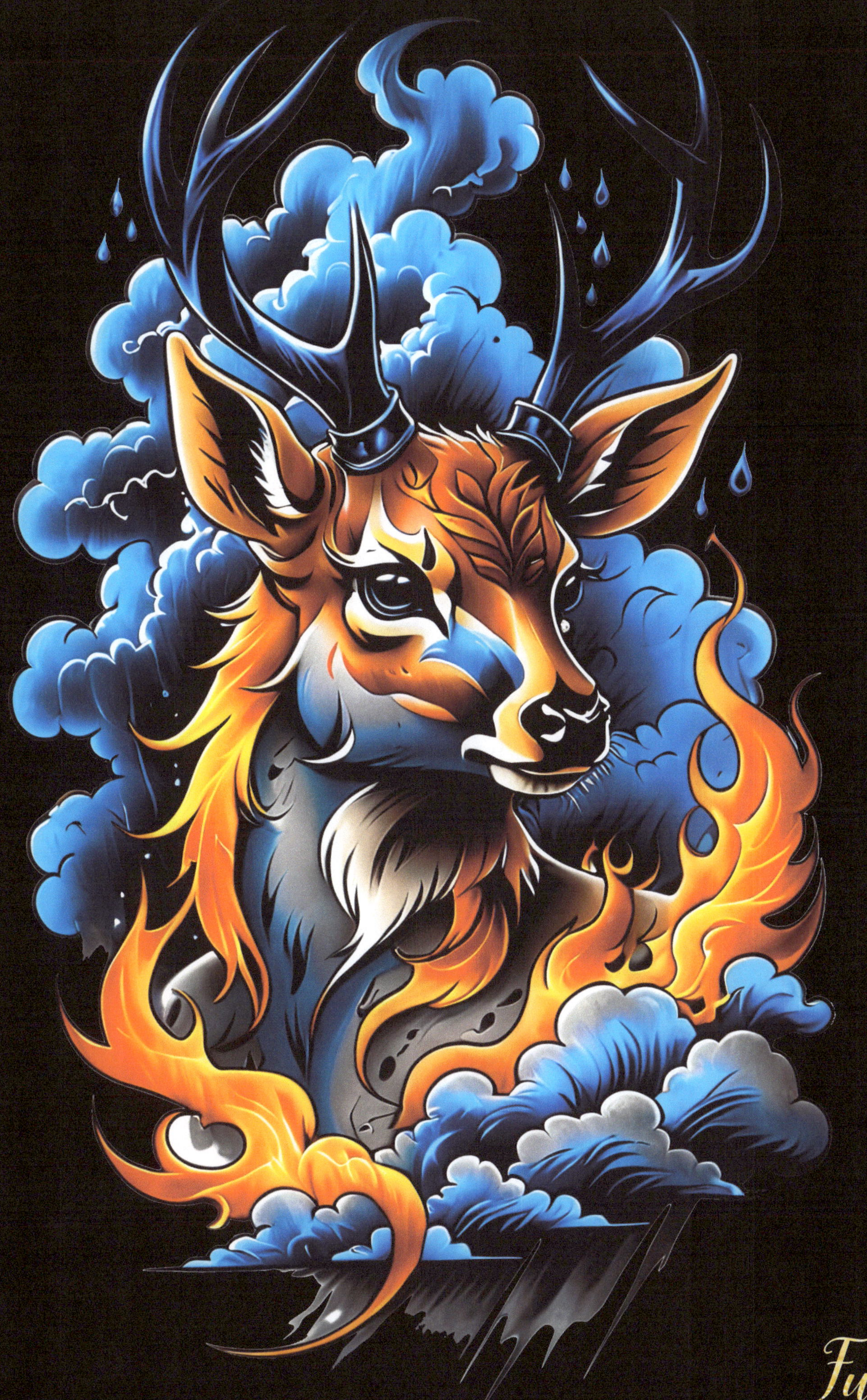

Furfur

Malphas

Malphas, the Grand President of Hell, is a formidable architect of infernal politics and demonic fortresses. Known for his cunning and capacity to deceive, Malphas is depicted with the sinister features of a crow, an animal often associated with foresight and guardianship in mythology but also with trickery and misfortune. His domain over the construction of impregnable fortresses and high towers symbolizes not only physical strength and security but also the strategic depths of deception and the isolation that power can create.

Symbolic Representation: Malphas's crow features—sharp eyes, a dark plume, and a commanding presence—perfectly encapsulate his role as a watchful overseer and a manipulator. These characteristics reflect his ability to observe from great heights, either literally atop the towers he constructs or metaphorically above the scheming of Hell's labyrinthine politics. His constructions, while serving as strongholds, also symbolize the barriers one builds around themselves with lies and deceit, illustrating the dual nature of protection and imprisonment.

Cultural Significance: Crows are often seen in various cultures as omens of change or as carriers of souls between the worlds of the living and the dead, adding a layer of spiritual and mystical depth to Malphas's character. In the context of demonology, Malphas's role as a builder of towers and fortresses can be interpreted as a metaphor for the structures of power and dominance that are erected within any political or social hierarchy. His presence serves as a reminder of the betrayal and manipulation that often accompany the pursuit of power, echoing cautionary tales of hubris and moral corruption throughout human history.

Artistic Elements: Artistically, Malphas can be envisioned overseeing vast, dark landscapes where the architecture is as oppressive as it is impressive—gigantic towers and fortresses with thick walls, shadowy corridors, and imposing gates, all designed to awe and intimidate. These structures might be adorned with gothic elements—gargoyles, arches, and spires—that further enhance their menacing aesthetic. The backdrop could be a twilight sky, perpetually on the verge between night and day, symbolizing the moral ambiguities of Malphas's dealings.

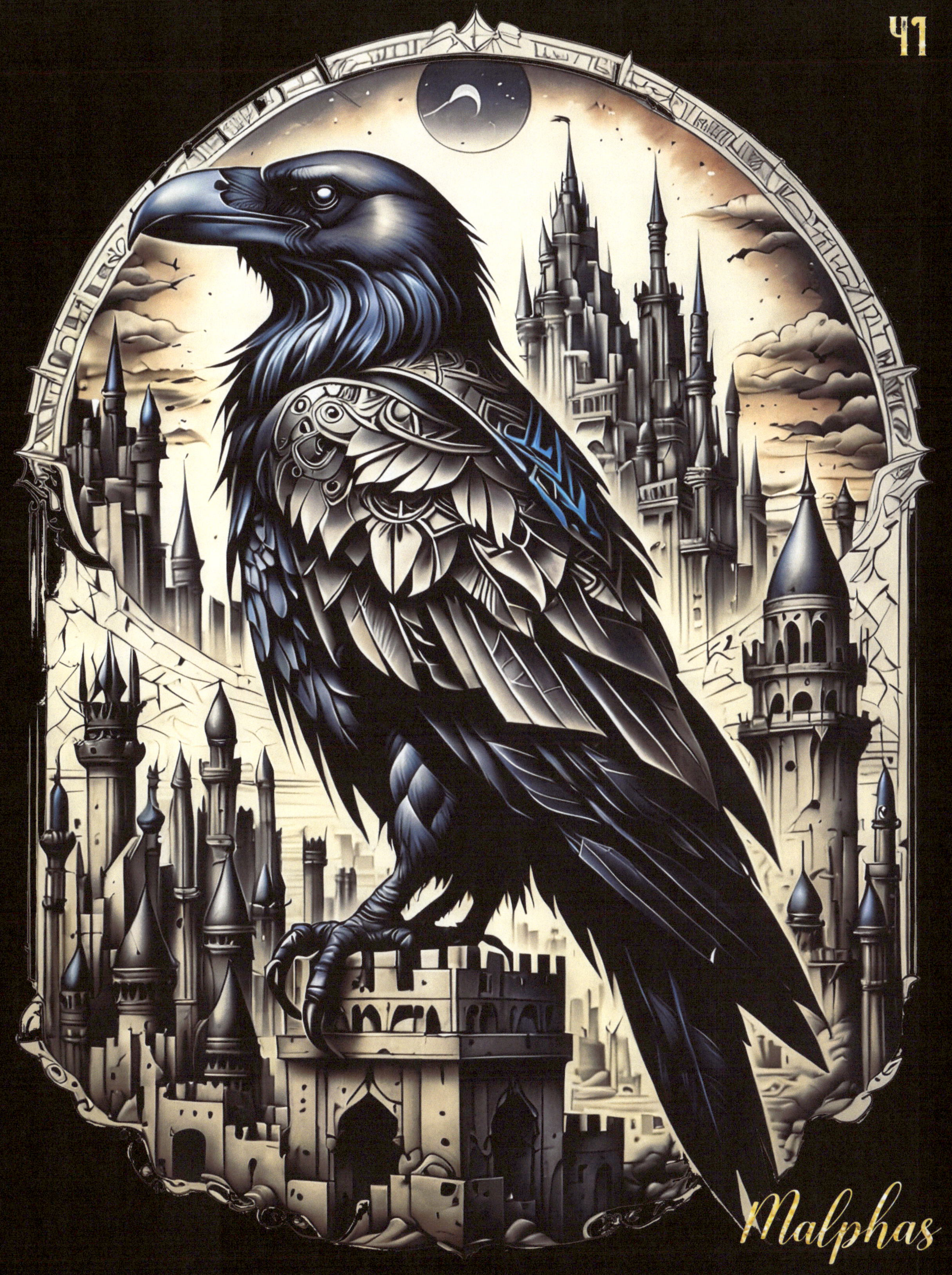
Malphas

Marchosias

Marchosias, known in the demonological lore as a formidable warrior demon, commands respect both in Hell and among those who evoke him. Described in the Pseudomonarchia Daemonum as a great and strong Duke, his depiction as a valiant wolf with dragon's wings that exhale blue flames encapsulates his ferocity and martial prowess. This figure not only symbolizes brute strength but also the valor needed to confront and conquer one's inner demons, making him a guardian of warriors and a patron for those facing personal battles.

Symbolic Representation: Marchosias's form—a wolf with the wings of a dragon—blends two powerful animal symbols. The wolf represents cunning, loyalty, and the ability to navigate complex social structures, while dragon wings signify transcendence, power, and a connection to ancient, mystic knowledge. The blue flames he exhales mark his speech and breath as impactful, with the color blue often associated with depth and stability, but also with cold fury and destructive potential. This combination portrays him as a creature of both earth and air, embodying the balance between intellect and instinct, thought and action.

Cultural Significance: In many traditions, wolves are seen as symbols of guidance and guardianship, while dragons are viewed as protectors of sacred treasures or profound secrets. Marchosias's dual aspect makes him a figure of spiritual and moral complexity, often called upon in medieval and Renaissance magic for his supposed truthfulness to his summoners and his ability to grant victories. He embodies the warrior's spirit—fearless and relentless in pursuit of truth and defense of the weak, reflecting the medieval knight's ideal and the samurai's code.

Artistic Elements: Artistically, Marchosias can be depicted in a dynamic, battle-ready stance, with his wings unfurled and his jaws parted in a fierce snarl, emitting those signature blue flames. The background could be a battlefield or a mythical landscape, adding an element of epic narrative to his portrayal. The flames not only illuminate his form but also cast a surreal glow that can highlight the mystical aspects of his nature. The use of stark contrasts between the dark shadows of his form and the bright light of his flames can dramatically emphasize his dual nature as a destructive force and a protective spirit.

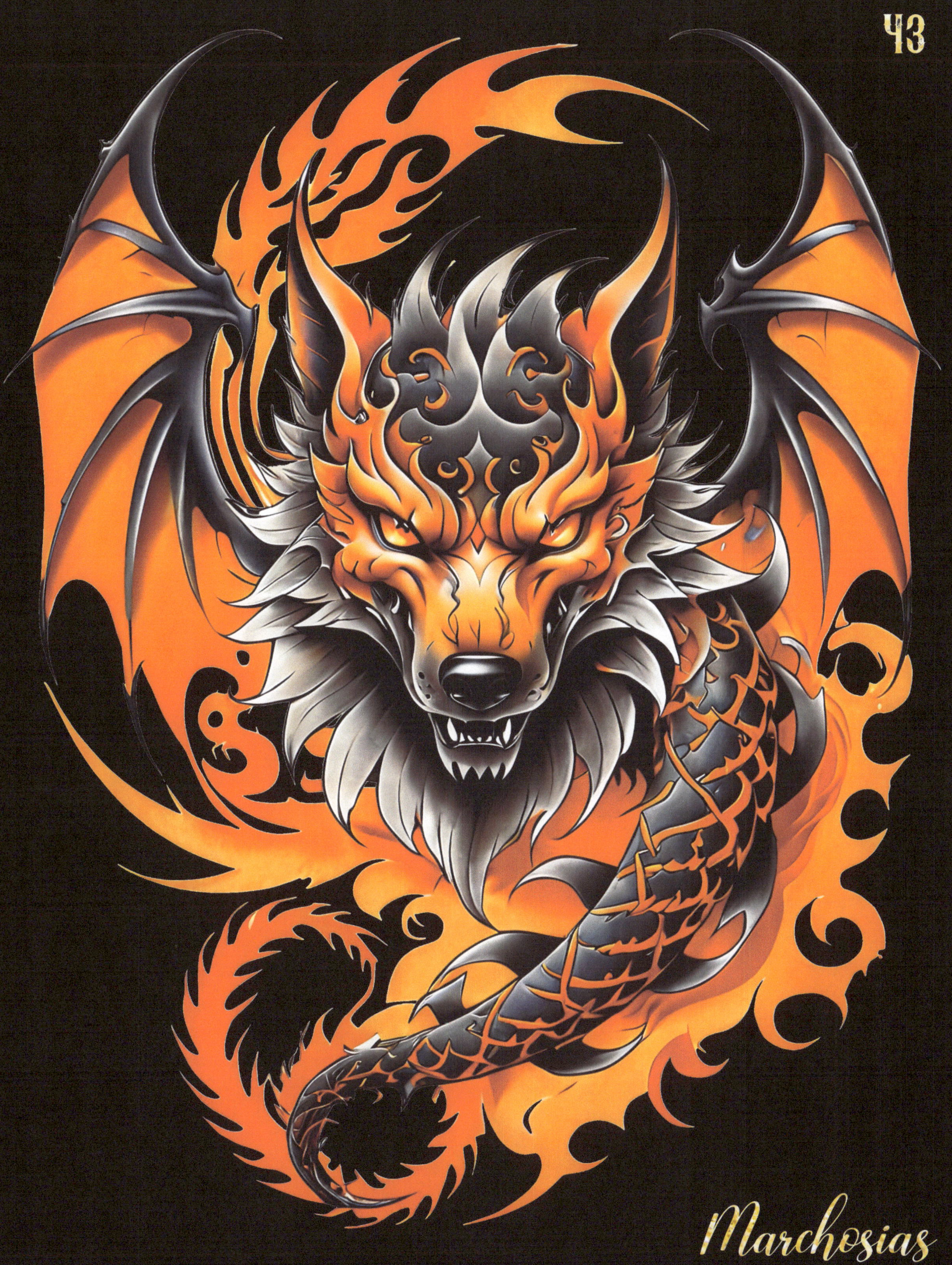

Marchosias

Zagan

Zagan, a demon known for his alchemical prowess, is celebrated and feared for his ability to transmute base substances into precious ones. As a figure who embodies the principle of metamorphosis, Zagan represents the profound and often unsettling changes that alchemy—both literal and metaphorical—can bring about. His power to turn wine into blood and coins into wine captures the essence of transformation, echoing the ancient pursuit of alchemy not just to change physical substances but also to evolve the human soul.

Symbolic Representation: Zagan is often depicted engaged in alchemical experiments, surrounded by flasks and scrolls, the air around him shimmering with the latent power of transmutation. This imagery highlights his mastery over the foundational elements of the universe, manipulating them to reveal the hidden potentials within. His ability to change wine into blood and vice versa symbolizes the life-giving and life-taking aspects of nature, reflecting on the dual nature of creation and destruction inherent in all change.

The depiction of Zagan performing these transformations can include intricate symbols and scripts from ancient alchemical texts, emphasizing the depth of knowledge required for such feats. These symbols also serve as a reminder of the spiritual and philosophical dimensions of alchemy, where the transformation of substances is akin to spiritual enlightenment and the quest for the philosopher's stone.

Cultural Significance: In historical and cultural contexts, alchemy is more than just the quest for turning lead into gold; it is a deeply symbolic process that reflects the human journey towards perfection and understanding. Zagan, as a demonic alchemist, challenges the natural order, pushing the boundaries of what is possible and questioning the limits imposed by the physical and spiritual laws. His actions can be seen as both revolutionary and heretical, embodying the tension between human ambition and cosmic law.

Artistic Elements: Artistically, Zagan can be envisioned in a richly detailed alchemist's laboratory, an environment that is both chaotic and ordered, where every tool and ingredient has a purpose. The atmosphere could be heavy with the scents of molten metals and pungent elixirs, visually represented by swirling mists and glowing substances. His figure, perhaps slightly obscured by the steam and vapors of his work, adds an element of mystery and focus on his transformative acts.

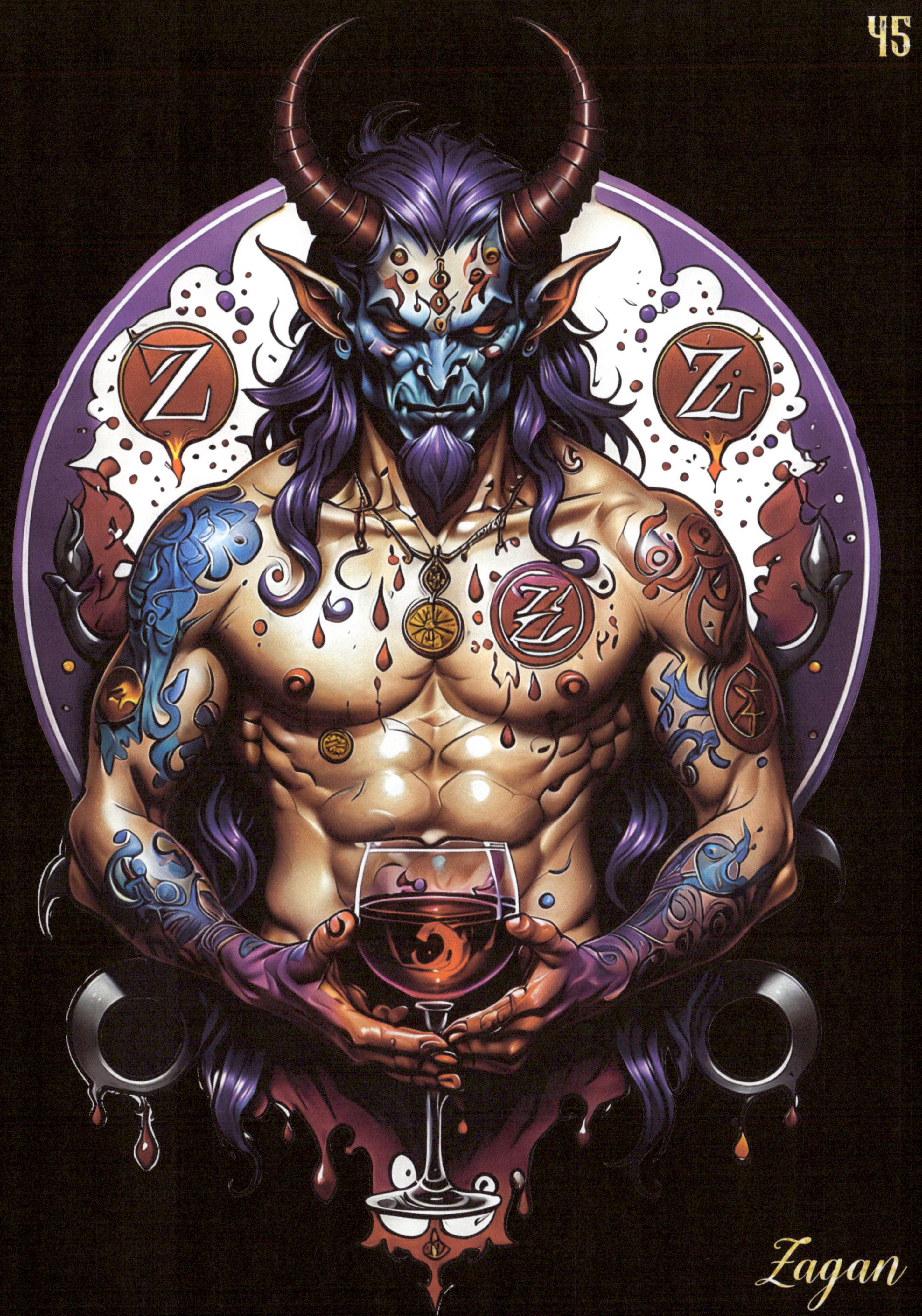

Zagan

Aamon

Aamon, also known as Amon or Amaymon, is a powerful demon whose attributes encapsulate the dual nature of his existence. Often depicted with the fearsome features of a wolf and the cunning of a serpent, Aamon straddles the line between beastly ferocity and calculating deception. This combination positions him as a formidable figure in demonic lore, not only as a purveyor of prophecy but also as an emblem of the nuanced pursuit of truth.

Symbolic Representation: Aamon's wolf and snake features symbolize his mastery over two very different realms of nature—the wild, untamed forests and the secretive, subterranean worlds. The wolf represents instinct, loyalty, and the strength of the pack, while the serpent symbolizes renewal, cunning, and the penetration of hidden truths. Together, they illustrate Aamon's ability to navigate and reconcile these forces within himself, offering insights that are both primal and profound.

This duality is central to Aamon's role as a demon of prophecy and truth. He embodies the internal conflicts that often accompany the search for knowledge—between base instincts and higher reasoning, between loyalty to one's group and the pursuit of personal enlightenment. His presence suggests that truth is not a singular, straightforward path but a complex journey that requires one to confront and integrate these conflicting aspects of self.

Cultural Significance: In many cultures, creatures like wolves and serpents are totemic symbols that appear in myths relating to the creation of the world, the foundation of knowledge, and the mysteries of the afterlife. Aamon's depiction with these features taps into a deep mythological vein, suggesting his ancient and elemental nature. As a demon of prophecy, he challenges individuals to look beyond mere appearances and to delve deeper into the metaphysical and moral questions that govern their lives.

Artistic Elements: Artistically, Aamon can be portrayed in an environment that reflects his complex nature. Imagine a scene divided into two distinct yet overlapping areas: one wild and wooded, echoing the wolf's domain, and the other dark and cavernous, reminiscent of the serpent's lair. This setting not only highlights his dual nature but also the symbolic journey one must undertake in the pursuit of truth.

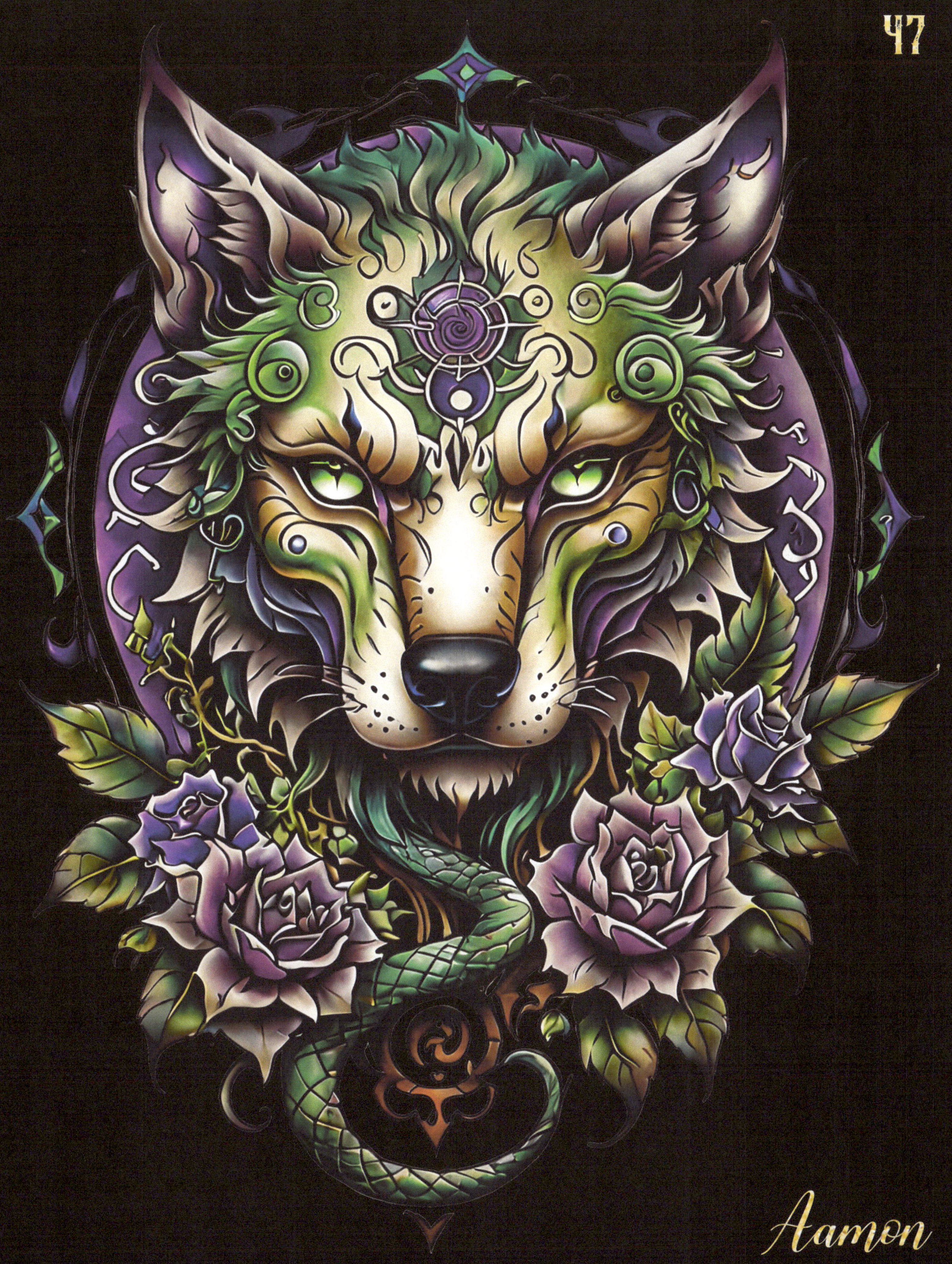

Aamon

Stolas

Stolas, often depicted as a princely figure within the demonic hierarchies of Hell, holds the title of the Prince of Astronomy. Known for his guise as a wise owl, Stolas bridges the natural world and the cosmos, revealing the intrinsic connections between earthly knowledge and celestial mysteries. This demon is not only a teacher of the stars but also a guardian of the secrets that plants—the fundamental elements of nature—hold within them.

Symbolic Representation: Stolas's portrayal as an owl embodies wisdom and vigilance, attributes traditionally associated with this bird across many cultures due to its keen sight in darkness and its solemn appearance. The owl's perspective symbolizes the ability to see beyond the deceits of time and space, to understand higher knowledge that spans the physical and the metaphysical realms. His connection to astronomy and the plants underscores his mastery over not just the celestial courses but also the earthly essences that dictate life's rhythms and secrets.

The integration of his form with plant motifs—perhaps feathers that subtly transition into leaves, or talons that resemble roots—further highlights his role as a mediator between sky and soil. This depiction not only enhances his mythical stature but also paints him as a creature of the universe's fabric, embodying the unity of all natural laws.

Cultural Significance: Owls hold a place of respect in many mythologies as symbols of wisdom and protectors of the sacred. Stolas's aspect as an owl who teaches about the stars and plants ties him to ancient traditions of herbalism and astrology, practices that seek to understand and harness the cosmos' energies for earthly benefits. In this sense, Stolas serves as a figure who challenges the boundaries between science and magic, making him a symbol of the age-old quest to decode the universe's mysteries.

Artistic Elements: Artistically, Stolas can be envisioned perched within a lush, verdant grove that borders on a celestial observatory, a setting that reflects his dual dominion over earth and sky. His feathers might shimmer with a celestial glow, speckled with starry patterns that echo the night sky, while his eyes could gleam with the luminescence of cosmic knowledge. Surrounding him, exotic plants and astrological instruments such as astrolabes and sextants might abound, each item rich with symbolic meaning and integrated into the natural setting.

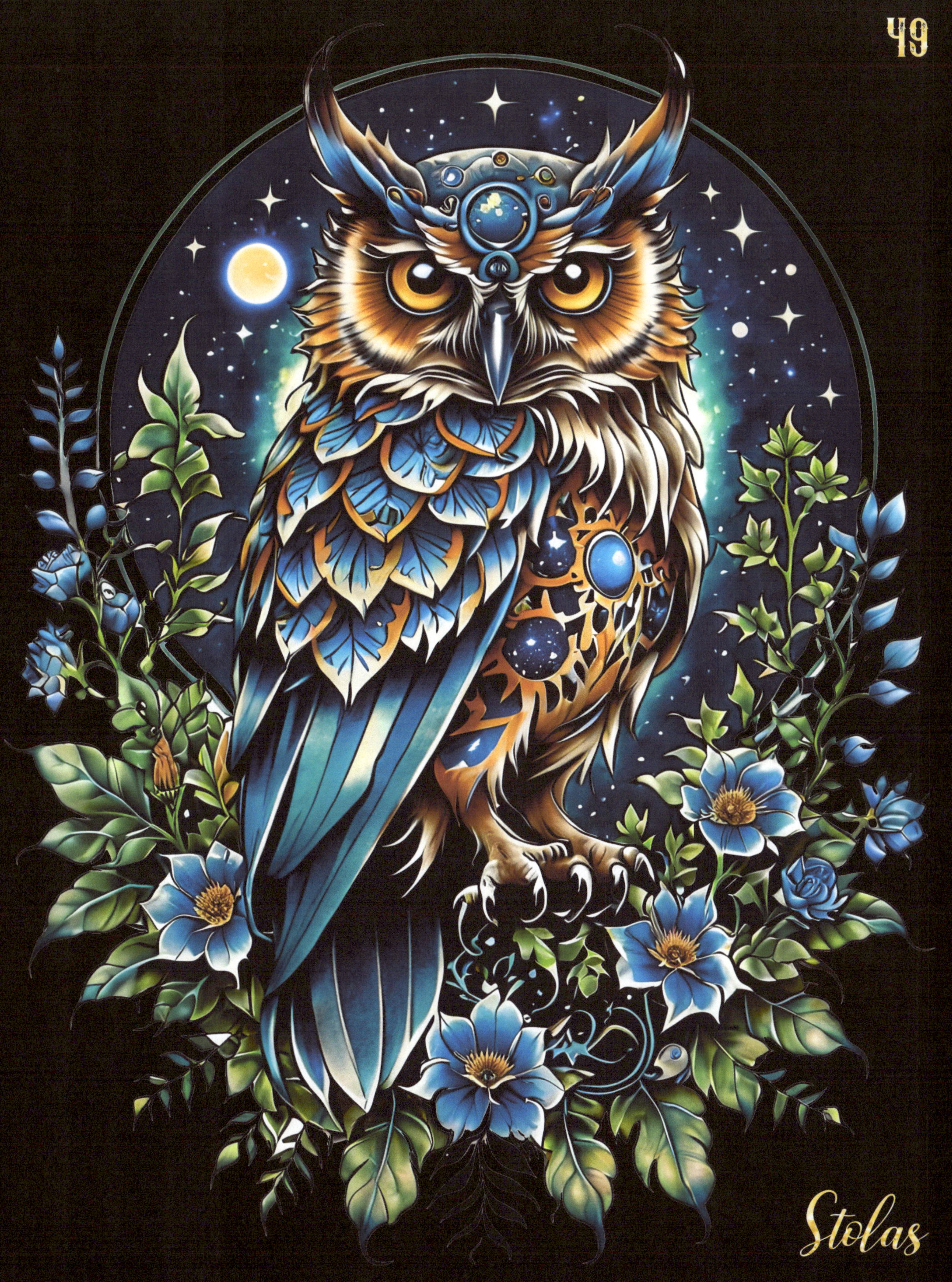
49
Stolas

Orobas

Orobas, a prince among demonic entities, stands out in the infernal hierarchy for his unwavering honesty and protective nature against deceit. Traditionally depicted as a majestic horse with a human face, Orobas represents a blend of nobility, strength, and intellect, embodying the virtues of truth and integrity in a realm often characterized by falsehood and manipulation.

Symbolic Representation: The form of Orobas as a horse with a human face is a powerful symbol intertwining the best qualities of both species: the horse's nobility, loyalty, and strength, and the human's intelligence and facial expressiveness, capable of nuanced communication and emotional connection. This depiction highlights Orobas's role as a forthright spirit, whose essence is to guide and protect those who seek the truth, offering clarity and insight in the face of deception and betrayal.

His portrayal often includes elements that emphasize his protective attributes, such as eyes that might glow with a clear, steadfast light, symbolizing his ability to see through darkness and deceit. His stance is firm and composed, reflecting his calm assurance and the stability he brings to those he aids.

Cultural Significance: In various mythologies, horses are creatures associated with freedom, power, and the crossing of boundaries between worlds, such as from life to death or from earth to heaven. The addition of a human face enhances this symbolism, infusing Orobas with the attributes of wisdom and guardianship, and making him a mediator between different realms of existence. This unique combination positions Orobas as a guide not only through physical journeys but also through spiritual or ethical dilemmas, embodying the pursuit of truth in a mythological context.

Artistic Elements: Artistically, Orobas can be depicted in a serene yet imposing manner, standing in a tranquil landscape that contrasts with the typical chaotic representations of other demonic figures. This setting could be a clear field under a wide and open sky, symbolizing openness and transparency, with Orobas himself illuminated by a beam of light that pierces through clouds—highlighting his connection to higher truths and divine protection.

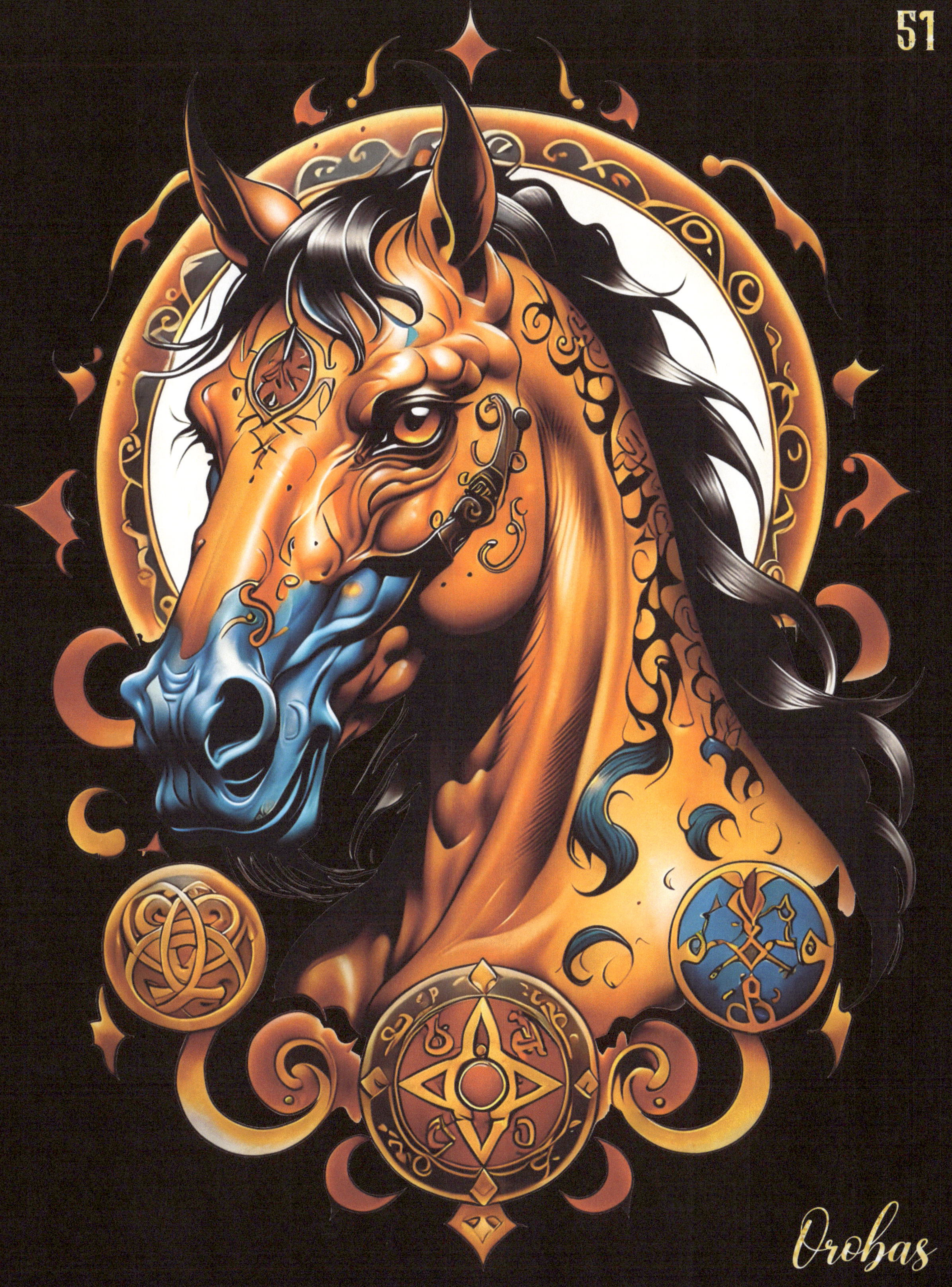

Orobas

Vepar

Vepar, a lesser-known but formidable demoness of the waters, holds dominion over the oceans and the dark secrets they envelop. Often depicted as a gruesome mermaid, Vepar combines the allure and danger of the sea in one being. Her control over maritime realms and her guidance of warships through treacherous waters highlight her dual role as both protector and destroyer, embodying the unpredictable and often perilous nature of the sea.

Symbolic Representation: Vepar's form as a mermaid with menacing features—scales that shimmer with the dark hues of the ocean depths and sharp, predatory teeth—serves as a vivid symbol of the sea's dual nature. The mermaid motif traditionally conjures images of beauty and enchantment, used to lure sailors to their doom. Vepar subverts this with her gruesome aspect, representing the real dangers of the sea—storms, whirlpools, and monsters lurking beneath the waves. Her appearance encapsulates the raw, untamed power of the ocean, a reminder of the respect and caution it demands.

Cultural Significance: Mermaids and sea monsters have occupied the tales of seafaring cultures across the globe, often embodying the mysteries and fears associated with vast, unexplored waters. Vepar's depiction taps into these ancient narratives, positioning her as a guardian of nautical secrets and a manifestation of the ocean's destructive potential. She is a figure of awe and fear, a deity-like embodiment of the sea's capricious spirit, commanding the natural forces that sailors and fishermen both revere and dread.

Artistic Elements: Artistically, Vepar can be portrayed amidst a dramatic seascape, where towering waves and swirling mists frame her formidable figure. Her scales might catch the fleeting light that filters down from the stormy surface, casting an eerie glow that illuminates her from within. This visual portrayal not only emphasizes her connection to the deep but also her role in guiding or misguiding naval vessels—she could be shown either calming the waters around a ship or summoning a storm against it.

Her surroundings might include elements that emphasize the ocean's mystery and danger—sunken ships, skeletal remains of drowned sailors, and scattered treasures from countless forgotten wrecks. These elements not only enhance the setting but also weave a narrative of the countless fates she has commanded.

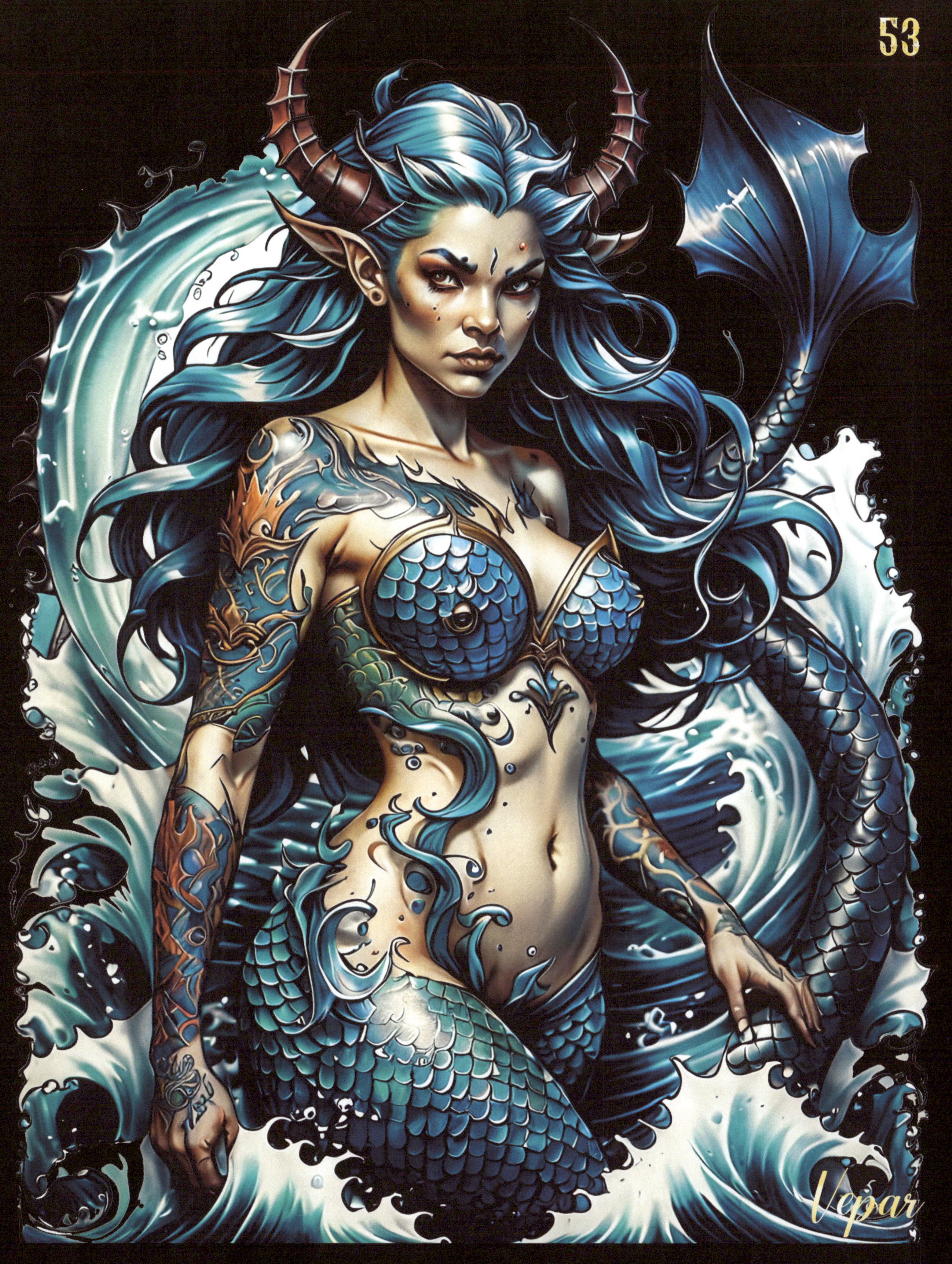
Vepar

Thank You for Your Purchase

On behalf of the entire team at Life Style Daily, we extend our deepest gratitude to you for choosing to explore the enigmatic realm of "Tatto Design Book - Demonology" Your interest in this unique collection not only supports our work but also enriches the ongoing dialogue between ancient symbolism and modern expression.

We Value Your Feedback

As we strive to provide content that captivates and enlightens, your feedback is invaluable to us. We invite you to share your experiences with "Infernal Ink"—whether it has inspired a new tattoo, provoked thought, or simply offered you a gateway into the profound symbolism of the demonic realms. Please consider leaving a review or reaching out to us directly with your insights and stories. Your input not only helps us improve but also connects and expands our community of like-minded enthusiasts.

Connect With Us

Join us on our journey by following Life Style Daily on our social media platforms, where we continue to explore the intersection of lifestyle, art, and spirituality. Engage with us and others in the community to discover, discuss, and delve deeper into the fascinating world of tattoos and their rich symbolic heritage.

Thank You, Once Again

We are truly honored to accompany you on your exploration of the infernal and the sublime. May the demons within these pages inspire you, challenge you, and guide you in your personal and artistic endeavors.

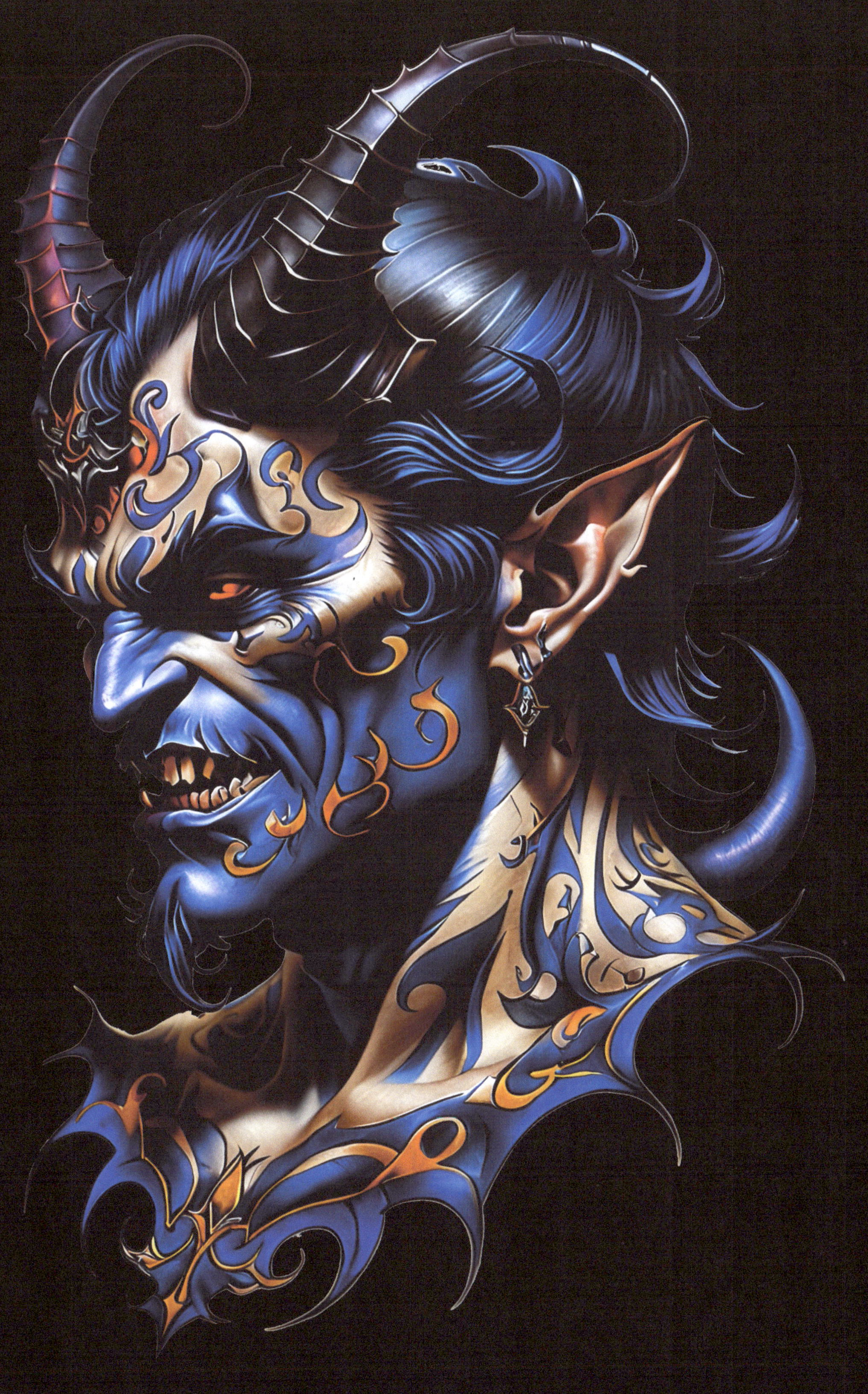